AF338264

"Page after page, Timothy Laurito provides truths from Scripture that are essential for Spirit-filled living. When endorsing a book, it's important to determine three things: (1) Does the author have something to say? (2) Does the author practice what they write about? And (3) Does the author have the right motivation? In *Pentecostal Perspectives*, Dr. Laurito checks all three boxes. This is a must-read resource for both the pastor and the parishioner."

—**DOUG CLAY**, general superintendent,
Assemblies of God USA

"Timothy Laurito's *Pentecostal Perspectives* ably demonstrates that a Pentecost experience of the Holy Spirit is not an isolated incident in the life of a believer but a way of approaching—and navigating—all of faith and practice in one's walk with Jesus Christ. He writes in an accessible and winsome style yet with biblical and theological substance. Anyone who has ever wondered, at least to themselves, 'What difference does Pentecost make for the Christian life?' will find this work helpful.

—**TONY RICHIE**, associate professor of theology,
Pentecostal Theological Seminary

"In *Pentecostal Perspectives*, Timothy Laurito offers a framework for thinking about Spirit-driven living that is much needed for our time. Combining exceptional scholarship with an approachable tone, this work is a blessing to the Pentecostal church as contemporary leaders seek to allow the Spirit to create new realities in their own lives first."

—**MIKE RAKES**, president,
Evangel University

"This timely new book comes in a season when many within the Western church struggle with identity issues. In *Pentecostal Perspectives*, Timothy Laurito makes a powerful case for what it means to be Pentecostal and what Spirit-filled living should look like."

—**SAMUEL RODRIGUEZ**, president,
National Hispanic Christian Leadership Conference

"Timothy Laurito has emerged as a leading academic voice within the Spirit-filled church. Yet the practical, relevant approach taken in *Pentecostal Perspectives* makes this rich text accessible to non-academicians as well."

—**KERMIT S. BRIDGES**, president,
Southwestern Assemblies of God University

Pentecostal Perspectives

Pentecostal Perspectives

A Guide for Faith and Practice

TIMOTHY LAURITO

Foreword by Tim Hill

WIPF & STOCK · Eugene, Oregon

PENTECOSTAL PERSPECTIVES
A Guide for Faith and Practice

Wipf & Stock
An Imprint of Wipf and Stock Publishers
199 W. 8th Ave., Suite 3
Eugene, OR 97401

www.wipfandstock.com

PAPERBACK ISBN: 978-1-6667-7663-8
HARDCOVER ISBN: 978-1-6667-7664-5
EBOOK ISBN: 978-1-6667-7665-2

07/28/23

For my mother, Marna Laurito (May 9, 1964–November 9, 2021).
Thank you for introducing me to Pentecostalism and for living a
Spirit-filled example before me.

Contents

Foreword

Pentecostalism has been part of Christianity since the disciples were filled with the Holy Spirit as described by Luke:

> When the day of Pentecost had come, they were all together in one place. And suddenly there came from heaven a noise like a violent rushing wind, and it filled the whole house where they were sitting. And there appeared to them tongues as of fire distributing themselves, and they rested on each one of them. And they were all filled with the Holy Spirit and began to speak with other tongues, as the Spirit was giving them utterance (Acts 2:1–4).

Most Pentecostals are aware of the modern-day history of the Pentecostal movement, which was launched during the 1906 Azusa Street Revival in Los Angeles. Evangelist William Seymour led an awakening that spread across the nation and eventually around the world. He and other disciples from Azusa, including G. B. Cashwell, took this fiery message to hungry believers, leading revivals that overflowed tents and meeting halls while at the same time sparking controversy among some established religious organizations. Pentecostal movements such as the Assemblies of God and the Church of God in Christ were birthed from Azusa. Others, such as the Church of God (Cleveland, Tennessee), embraced the Pentecostal experience when top leaders were gloriously filled with the Holy Spirit.

Today, those who call themselves Pentecostal number over 650 million. It is a spiritual force that fills some of the largest edifices and attracts massive gatherings every single week. Yet, while contemporary Pentecostalism has been around for more than 100 years, it is still a relatively new movement compared to the mainstream groups of Christendom like Catholics, Lutherans, Episcopalism, Baptists, and Methodists. These groups have deep roots in their doctrinal and theological beliefs, with volumes of texts and commentaries to back up centuries of thought.

For those who live the Pentecostal lifestyle, there is a level of trust in the guidance from the third person of the Trinity. We rely on inspiration and revelation perhaps more than the traditional Christian. However, as a movement this trust can bring a greater possibility for misinterpretation of scriptural principles. While divine inspiration should not be discounted, there is merit in addressing the core principles of the Christian life through a Pentecostal lens: the *Pentecostal perspective*.

Chapters in this book tackle some of the most critical and fundamental elements of Christianity, all with a Holy Spirit underpinning. How does a biblical worldview differ among Pentecostals? Where in Scripture is the Holy Spirit revealed to transform our worldview? How does being baptized in the Holy Spirit affect witnessing to the ungodly society around us? Does being Spirit-filled impact the way the Pentecostal expresses praise and worship? How does a Pentecostal approach to the practice of prayer differ from other mainline Christian groups? Each of these questions reveals that Pentecostalism is much more than a group that speaks in tongues; it is a dynamic movement that centers its faith and practice on living in the Spirit. The final chapters include perspectives on what could be loosely claimed as unique Pentecostal topics: spiritual disciplines and spiritual gifts. These crucial characteristics have come to define what it means to be a dedicated, lifelong Pentecostal. As people who take the Spirit working in our world seriously, Pentecostals emphasize the vital need for spiritual empowerment in this present age. A total dependency upon the Spirit is the hallmark of Pentecostal ministry, from helping ascertain the Spirit's will to enabling and equipping ministry callings.

Those of us who claim this gift of being Spirit-filled (and thus, Pentecostal) don't need convincing that our perspectives on spiritual matters can seem, at times, divinely inspired. We may even claim superiority in our access to the Father because of a relationship with the Holy Spirit. However, like any other Christ-centered movement, Pentecostalism requires guidance and a proper perspective based on scriptural principles.

Dr. Laurito strives to provide such a perspective in this book. This book will broaden and deepen your thinking about what it means to be Pentecostal. May everyone blessed to call themselves Pentecostal be receptive to Spirit-led training as they read. My prayer is that this resource would help keep Pentecostalism on a strategic path to finishing the Great Commission.

Dr. Tim Hill
General Overseer
Church of God

Introduction

A change in perspective is powerful. Interestingly, it only takes a little information to completely shift our perspective. For example, imagine you are on a plane flying from Dallas to Cleveland for work. No sooner than the seat belt sign is turned off your attention is drawn to a family seated in front of you. You notice them because two little boys dart from their seats and begin jumping up and down in the aisle. Like wildfire, they start spreading chaos all around you. All the while, the parents seem oblivious to what is happening.

> "Parents today are so irresponsible," you tell the person sitting next to you.
>
> Nodding in agreement, they comment, "If I were those parents, I would never let my kids act this way."
>
> You can't help but feel your frustrations rising as the kids kick the seats and fight with one another. "Something has to be done," you burst out, making sure you say it loud enough for everyone to hear your complete disgust.
>
> Just as you are about to signal for the flight attendant, the father of the unruly children turns around. Holding a baby, the exhausted-looking father says, "I'm so sorry my boys are acting out. We just found out our infant daughter has an inoperable brain tumor."
>
> Choking back tears, the father explains, "We are headed to the Mayo Clinic in Cleveland to try an experimental treatment. We've been cooped up in a hospital all week, so the boys are struggling to be still."

What has changed? Nothing and everything at the same time. The two unruly boys are still wound up, letting off energy like little rockets, but your perspective has suddenly changed. Now, instead of feeling anger and resentment, you feel compassion and empathy. Why? Because a change in perspective can completely alter the way we think and act. A change in perspective can be significant due to its ability to guide us into a deeper appreciation of a situation and offer new insights about living in this world.

The purpose of this book is to introduce essential theological themes and then show what a Pentecostal perspective adds to the subject. The objective is to provide the reader with a clearer understanding of the unique perspectives Pentecostalism contributes to the Christian life. For the Pentecostal, my desire is for you to discover new depths to your experience in the Spirit. For the non-Pentecostal, my hope is that you would come to appreciate the Pentecostal's contribution to what it means to live in the Spirit. The Pentecostal emphasis on the ongoing empowering work of the Holy Spirit in this present age is a perspective with much to offer modern Christendom.

The book aims to bridge the divide between Pentecostal academia and the Pentecostal pew. My observation has been that the academy and the average churchgoer tend to operate in separate silos with little effort made to connect them. This book offers scholarly footnotes and additional recommended reading at the end of each chapter. However, the tone of the book is conversational and approachable.

Each chapter first presents a theological subject and explains the issue's overall significance. Next, the theme is examined from a Pentecostal perspective to discover what contributions Pentecostalism brings to the topic. Finally, each chapter ends with application questions about the content, and some suggested reading if you want to go deeper on the subject. The purpose of the application questions is to provide the reader with the opportunity to meditate on how the biblical truths presented could be practically implemented in their life. One of the central perspectives of Pentecostalism is the belief that theology must go beyond the theoretical—but through the Spirit—to become integrated into the life of the Christian.

Finally, I want to clarify that by presenting a Pentecostal perspective, I am not claiming to represent all perspectives within Pentecostalism. Since there are nearly 650 million Pentecostal adherents worldwide, it would be unwise to assume the content of this book describes all Pentecostals and their perspectives on matters. Like any group of this size, one should expect great diversity within Pentecostal thought. It has been noted that a range of Pentecostalism exists that is varied in its expressions and identity.[1] Thus,

---

1. Anderson, *Introduction to Pentecostalism*, 2.

my goal is merely to provide a broad lens that focuses on the general thinking Pentecostals possess regarding the task of living a Spirit-filled life.

Whether you are new to Pentecostalism or have a long history with Pentecostal perspectives, I pray God would deepen your understanding and application of these Spirit-inspired truths. I echo Paul's prayer to the Ephesians as you read this book,

> That the God of our Lord Jesus Christ, the Father of glory, may give you the Spirit of wisdom and of revelation in the knowledge of him, having the eyes of your hearts enlightened, that you may know what is the hope to which he has called you, what are the riches of his glorious inheritance in the saints (Eph 6:17–18).

1

Perspectives on a Biblical Worldview

All Christian experience in this era must be properly "Pentecostal"—that is, shaped by the experience of Pentecost, the outpouring of the Spirit on the church.

—Craig Keener

INTRODUCTION

A young boy noticed his grandfather had fallen asleep on the living room chair. As he watched his sleeping grandfather, a mischievous thought burst into the little boy's head. Quietly running to the kitchen, the lad opened the fridge and got a piece of stinky Limburger cheese. As silently as possible, the boy gently placed the cheese in his grandpa's mustache and then patiently waited for his prank to work.

> "Why does this room stink?" the grandfather asked, rousing from his sleep.
>
> Getting up and going to the kitchen to investigate the smell, the grandfather proclaimed, "It stinks in here as well!"
>
> Deciding he needed some fresh air, the frustrated grandfather stepped outside and, to his surprise, announced, "The whole world stinks!"

The grandfather's smell of the "whole world" was influenced by a piece of stinky cheese that was going with him everywhere he went. Much like the story illustrates, a worldview is something that goes with us and influences the way we perceive the world.

For the Christian, one of the most essential elements of maintaining faith is cultivating a biblical way of viewing the world. Developing an approach to our world that is filtered through Scripture is critical because it helps to shape one's understanding of the events in our world, our place in it, and our ultimate purpose. At the heart of shaping the Christian's worldview is Holy Scripture. The Christian views the Word of God as much more than a religious text that offers moral principles; it is *the* guide for faith and practice. This means the faith of the Christian must have the words and works of Christ as its basis for what they believe about God's working in this world. As such, it should be the goal of every Christian to read and study Scripture for the purpose of cultivating a value system that is consistent with the teachings of God's Word.[1]

As meditative literature, Scripture is designed to do more than provide its readers with ancient narratives or historical correspondences by early church apostles. Instead, Scripture is ultimately designed to fundamentally transform its reader's perspectives as it reshapes the Christian's thinking and sanctifies the believer "in truth; Your word is truth" (John 17:17). This transformation can only take place through a person immersing themselves in Scripture and allowing its divine truth to cut through opposing truth claims and "judge the thoughts and intentions of the heart" (Heb 4:12).

With the rise of the modern secular society, ungodly beliefs and behaviors have continued to choke out a biblical perspective. Like a boa constrictor, ever so slowly, an ungodly worldview has squeezed out a biblical worldview from the American public consciousness.[2] Almost without warning, we now find ourselves fully immersed in a post-Christian society. In virtually every area of modern culture, the postmodern worldview has unashamedly assaulted biblical philosophies and done whatever possible to destroy any traces of divine truth. Not only this, but some within Christendom have begun to adopt the same unbiblical perspectives as the secular culture, leaving the modern church at a critical crossroads.

Within this cultural context, the twenty-first-century Pentecostal finds themselves faced with a unique opportunity. Perhaps, since the beginning of Pentecostalism, there has never been a time in which the Pentecostal's perspective on a biblical worldview can shine more brightly than it can in our current culture.

1. Anderson, Clark, and Naugle, *Introduction to Christian Worldview*, 2.
2. Naugle, *Worldview*, 4.

BIBLICALLY COLORED GLASSES

Before understanding the significance and distinctions of a biblical worldview, it is essential to define the term in its more general sense. At the risk of oversimplification, a worldview is the lens through which a person views the world around them. A worldview is like a set of colored glasses that influences our perceptions and shades everything we see in the world. By controlling our assessment of reality, a worldview impacts our thoughts, values, and decisions.

An estimated 2.2 billion people in the world currently need corrective lenses. Perhaps, like myself, you fall into the category of depending on some visual aid to see the world around you. For so many who struggle with poor eyesight, their view of the world is dependent on ensuring they regularly get their vision checked. Much like one's natural vision, a person's philosophies and belief systems must be evaluated to ensure they are not mistakenly following false ideas, values, or passions. The fascinating thing about a worldview is that it is constantly being shaped and colored as we perceive and contemplate our existence. The way a person views the world is "put on" every moment of a person's life as they navigate through the culture around them. These colored lenses are so intrinsically natural to our existence that many people (even Christians) are blind to how their perspectives tint their thinking, judgments, and actions.

A worldview is like a set of colored glasses that influences our perceptions and shades everything we see in the world.

Further, a worldview is not a static or stationary thing. This means the lenses through which we perceive the world are constantly being reshaded by the stimulus we encounter. The color of our worldview lenses can change and adjust throughout our life. While these shifts in philosophy and perspective can occur very rapidly, they often happen gradually, sometimes so slowly that we are even unaware that they have changed. Whether a worldview changes quickly or very slowly, the thing that should concern us is the fact that it is changeable. The simple fact that our value systems and views of the world can change should cause us to continually examine our worldview to ensure that it is consistent with Scripture. In a real sense, the person who fails to examine their value systems is doubly blind.

Picture the absurdity of a person that could not see being completely unaware that they have no eyesight. In a real sense, they would be blind to their blindness. Undoubtedly, the challenges of navigating through this world without any sight would be complex enough, but compounding the issues by being unaware of their condition would be far worse. While the idea of a blind person not perceiving their blindness may seem ridiculous from a physical perspective, tragically, it is the condition of many people's spiritual condition. However, the Christian should not live this way or suffer from spiritual blindness for they are called to use the lens of Scripture to ensure they see things from an eternal perspective.

Christ used the illustration of double-blindness to refer to those who followed the religious hypocrisy of the Pharisees. Stuck in religious traditions, the Pharisees could not see how their man-made rules had so distorted their worldview away from biblical principles. Worse yet, Jesus revealed that those who followed the teachings of the blind Pharisees were themselves in the dark to the fact they were being led by spiritually blind people. Referring to the spiritual sightlessness of both the Pharisees and their followers, Jesus said,

> Leave them alone; they are blind guides of blind people. And if a
> person who is blind guides another who is blind, both will fall into
> a pit (Matt 15:14).

Unquestionably, the consequences associated with possessing an unexamined worldview can lead to devastation ends.

At this point, it is critical to see there is a pit on both sides of a biblical worldview. On one side is the pit that I will call the Unreligious Unbiblical Worldview. While this pit is mired in ungodly thinking, it does not hide its opposition to biblical values. It openly promotes (even celebrates) its anti-biblical philosophies without any pretense or remorse. However, on the other side is a pit I will call the Religious Unbiblical Worldview. This pit consists of religious traditions and spiritual-looking activity, but it too falls from the path of a biblical worldview. However, the distinguishing aspect of this pit is that the muck here prefers to fancy itself as being spiritual. Yet, despite the religious labels that might be attached, any deviation from the solid foundation of Scripture will result in the same end, spiritual destruction. Given the cost associated with falling into either unbiblical ditch, every Christian must use the light of Scripture to guide them on the path of a biblical worldview (Ps 119:105).

As part of any vision exam, the optometrist will use a Snellen chart (the big E chart) to judge the vision of the patient. This chart was developed in order for there to be a standard measurement for determining a person's ability to see. For the Christian, the spiritual Snellen chart is none other than the Word of God. Scripture must be the standard by which the Christian judges their ability to properly see the world around them.

The non-Christian may construct their ideologies and value systems using a variety of ungodly lenses and have an ever-increasing number of standards they use to judge the correctness of their worldview. For the Christian, Scripture must remain the ultimate source for judging the value and validity of their belief system as they practice a lifestyle in which "the word of Christ richly dwell" (Col 3:16). Scripture is so fundamental for constructing the Christian's outlook on life that one cannot have a Christian worldview apart from possessing a biblical worldview.

Therefore, it could be said that the degree to which we possess a Christian worldview is the degree to which Scripture impacts our beliefs and behaviors. Further, since the human worldview is comprehensive—impacting every area of life—the Christian's value system is one that has the Bible influencing the entire framework of existence. In short, a biblical worldview guides and shapes every aspect of the Christian's thinking. When this happens, the Christian views life through biblically colored glasses.

A NEW CREATURE

If this is the case, then a biblical worldview is more than a set of religious beliefs confined to a doctrinal statement or the four corners of a church building. But in a real sense, a biblical philosophy and perspective is the lens through which the Christian thinks about everything within creation. Thus, the goal of cultivating a biblical value system is to train the thinking of the Christian to conform to Scripture through a continually transforming and "renewing of your mind" (Rom 12:2). Developing a biblical way of viewing the world requires the believer's mind be trained, informed, and equipped to handle information around them and filter it through the lens of Scripture.

Any philosophy or belief system is biblical *only* to the degree to which it is consistent with Scripture. It is the height of spiritual immaturity to naively trust that every view posited by a professing Christian is biblical for we are warned to "not believe every spirit" (1 John 4:1). Given the grave consequences associated with following unbiblical worldviews, the serious Christian is wise to study Scripture for themselves so they can accurately discern between a biblical belief system and a non-biblical way of viewing a given subject.

The first step in developing a biblical view of the world is straightforward but essential: to possess a biblical perspective, a person must come to saving faith in Christ. To cultivate a biblical mindset apart from saving faith in Christ is impossible. The apostle Paul explains this by revealing the mind controlled by ungodly passions is at war against the Spirit and will never submit to biblical philosophies, "for it is not even able to do so" (Rom 8:7). But upon salvation, the Spirit begins a work of sanctification, redeeming the mind of the Christian and transforming their worldview into one that is biblical.

Having come to saving faith in Christ, the transformation of a person's way of thinking from an ungodly way of thinking to a biblical worldview is a work of the Spirit in unity with the will of the Christian. Fundamental in developing a biblical value system is to allow the Spirit to cultivate both a mindset and a "willset."[3] While the Spirit is responsible for guiding and nurturing our minds toward a biblical worldview, the Christian does not sit by inactive in this process. Instead, the Christian is called to "set their minds on things of the Spirit" (Rom 8:6) and to "be renewed in the spirit of your mind and put on the new self" (Eph 4:22). Additionally, Paul admonishes Christians to be on guard against ungodly thinking that would seek to take believers "captive through philosophy and empty deception" (Col 2:8). Not only this, but Scripture instructs the Christian to have a mind that is prepared (1 Pet 1:13), mature (1 Cor 14:20), humble (Phil 2:5–8), and set on eternal matters (Col 3:2). These scriptures reveal an action of the human will is required of the follower of Christ to possess such a perspective.

Many Christians presume they have a biblical worldview simply because of their proximity to religious morality.[4] However, it is crucial to differentiate between familiarity with religiosity from personal integration of biblical truths. It is not enough to merely educate the Christian on biblical truth (unquestionably, we should do this). There must be an incorporation of a biblical way of thinking that goes beyond correct beliefs (orthodoxy)

3. Phillips, William, and Stonestreet, *Making Sense of Your World*, xii.

4. Smith, *Developing a Biblical Worldview*, 4.

to include correct behavior (orthopraxy). The purpose of the new birth is a radical renovation of the entire person (including their worldview). But this transformation is not merely theoretical but is "worked out" as the Christian allows the Spirit to alter their philosophies and perspectives to conform to Scripture (Phil 2:12).

The process of transforming the believer's worldview—from being hostile to God to being biblical—begins immediately upon conversion. However, it is a mistake to suppose that simply because someone comes to Christ they will quickly come to possess a biblical way of thinking. While certainly the work of the Spirit at conversion brings about a transformation of spiritual life (Eph 2:1–5) and a new life in Christ (2 Cor 5:17), this does not mean the stains of the former life of sin upon the mind are easily (or quickly) transformed. Instead, the new convert is expected to begin a journey of sanctification of their mindset and "willset." The Pentecostal sees the Spirit-inspired renovation of worldview as being essential for the new believer to grow in their spiritual maturity.

A PENTECOSTAL PERSPECTIVE

Pentecostal thinking begins with the Spirit. That is to say, the Pentecostal lens through which they experience the world is colored by the Spirit. For the Pentecostal, the framework for what it means to be a follower of Christ is mediated through a baptism *in* and experience *with* the Spirit. As such, a Pentecostal perspective on a biblical worldview sees

> **The foundation of Pentecostal thinking begins with the Spirit. That is to say, the Pentecostal lens through which they experience the world is "colored" by the Spirit.**

the Spirit as an indispensable aid in the formation of a biblical worldview. The Spirit invites Christians to embrace a biblical worldview and then empowers them in the continual application of scriptural truth. Likewise, the Pentecostal desires that the work of the Spirit be evident in the transformation of their whole being by bringing "life to your mortal bodies through His Spirit who dwells in you" (Rom 8:11).

In this way, Pentecostals relate their present experience with Scripture, to stories and events in the Bible, and then interpret and authenticate their present experience back through what they have read.[5] To be sure, there are errors to be avoided within this approach. However, there is something powerful about a hermeneutic that takes seriously Scripture's ability to speak into our present world. This means a Pentecostal biblical worldview begins with the assumption that Scripture has something to say about how modern Christians should view their current culture.

A Pentecostal perspective on a biblical worldview is more than a dogma to be followed but flows from a relationship with the Spirit. It is precisely this experience with the Spirit that provides the filter for the Pentecostal's perspectives. While the Pentecostal is christocentric in their understanding of the gospel, at the same time, they view the work of the Spirit as essential for living in a Christlike manner. While the implication of this is varied, for our purposes, this means the Pentecostal views the Spirit as indispensable for practically living out a biblical way of life. The Pentecostal takes seriously the idea that the Spirit can guide them toward a biblical worldview for they recognize that one of the primary purposes of the Spirit's arrival is that "He will guide you into all truth" (John 16:13). Further, to aid the Christian in living out biblical truth, the Pentecostal emphasizes the importance of Jesus' promise that "you will receive power when the Holy Spirit has come upon you" (Acts 1:8).

In outlining what makes a Pentecostal worldview distinct, Pentecostal philosopher James K. A. Smith offers five key elements:

> (1) radical openness to God; (2) enchanted theology of creation and culture; (3) a nondualistic affirmation of embodiment and materiality; (4) an affective, narrative epistemology; and (5) an eschatological orientation to mission and justice.[6]

Allow me to quickly restate Smith's list: (1) As a person who is comfortable with experiences in the Spirit, the Pentecostal is keenly aware that God's presence can (and often does) come expectantly; (2) the Pentecostal recognizes there is much more to the universe than physically observable, (3) the Pentecostal offers a holistic approach to the Spirit's work in this world that views the health of the body and material blessings as gifts from God; (4) the Pentecostal worldview gathers its knowledge about the working of the

---

5. Vondey, *Pentecostal Theology*, 16.

6. Smith, *Thinking in Tongues*, 32.

Spirit from the use of narrative; from Luke's narrative of the early church to the present-day church, Pentecostalism consists of stories; and (5) the Pentecostal perspective is guided by its belief that the Spirit has been poured out "in the last days" (Acts 2:17). Whatever else a Pentecostal worldview might be, it is evident it offers a perspective that sees the God of Scripture as being active in this present world through the Spirit.

The Pentecostal worldview sees the Spirit as an active force throughout Scripture. From creation (Gen 1:2) to the early church (Acts 2:4) to our future hope (Rev 22:17), the Spirit is moving with signs and wonders. Astonishingly, these signs and wonders performed by the Spirit are often done in partnership with believers (2 Cor 12:12; Acts 2:43; 14:3; Rom 15:19; Heb 2:4). Given this reality, a Pentecostal perspective of the Spirit prioritizes this collaborative partnership between the Spirit and believers to advance the kingdom of God in this world. It is this fundamental perspective that has caused Pentecostalism to be a powerful missionary movement throughout its storied history. To this point Pentecostal missiologist Paul Pomerville writes,

> The view of the Pentecostal movement as a missionary phenomenon is, in a sense, a manifestation of the very present and powerful kingdom of God in action. For it is evidence of the dynamic, redemptive activity of God the Holy Spirit in contemporary times.[7]

In other words, a Pentecostal perspective on a biblical worldview does not view Scripture as being merely an ancient text devoid of modern relevance. Instead, the Pentecostal sees the abrupt ending to the Acts of the Apostles as an invitation to continue the same mission through the same power that animated the early church.

Embedded within a Pentecostal way of thinking is an inherent understanding that one of the primary reasons the Spirit is needed today is to aid Christians in living out a biblical worldview. Surrounded by an ungodly society that promotes an endless array of unbiblical philosophies and values, the Pentecostal sees the Spirit as an indispensable guide to ensuring our beliefs and values continue to direct us on the "ways of life" (Acts 2:28).

As the movement that popularized the term "spiritual warfare," Pentecostalism is no stranger to the capabilities of evil spirits in shaping unbiblical worldviews.[8] Given this familiarity with fighting against unbiblical ideologies and values, the Pentecostal is uniquely positioned to engage

---

7. Pomerville, *Third Force in Missions*, 38.

8. Warren, "Spiritual Warfare," 286.

in ungodly influences in this present world (Eph 6:10–18). As such, the modern Pentecostal should be willing to identify and rebuke satanic agendas found in unbiblical philosophies. The twenty-first-century Pentecostal must not be fearful of denouncing ungodly spirits within the culture and of boldly proclaiming that "every spirit that does not confess Jesus is not from God; this is the spirit of the antichrist" (1 John 4:3). Further, the Pentecostal must reject ungodly philosophies that deny God's existence and have been "raised up against the knowledge of God" (2 Cor 10:5).

Equipped with the authority of Scripture and empowered by the anointing of the Spirit, the Pentecostal is uniquely qualified to live out a biblical worldview. As the embodied testimony of the Spirit, the modern Pentecostal has a responsibility to present a biblical value system to this generation so they may proclaim what those on the day of Pentecost stated: "we hear them in our own tongues speaking of the mighty deeds of God" (Acts 2:11).

CONCLUSION

Christians must cultivate a biblical worldview because it provides a framework for understanding and interpreting the world and informs beliefs and behaviors. For the Christian, the Holy Scriptures serve as the basis for their belief systems and values, and it must be studied and meditated upon in order to transform their thinking and align their beliefs and actions with the will of God. Without a biblical worldview, the Christian runs the risk of being influenced by secular and unbiblical ideologies that when followed will produce disastrous results. Therefore, it is essential for Christians to perpetually analyze and reshade the way they view the world through the lens of Scripture in order to ensure that every aspect of their thinking is consistent with biblical principles.

From a Pentecostal perspective, it is the work of the Holy Spirit that is indispensable in transforming the Christian's worldview. A Pentecostal worldview sees the Holy Spirit as the active force throughout the Word of God, from creation to our hope for the future, directing and initiating believers toward godly beliefs and behaviors. In summary, a Pentecostal perspective on a biblical worldview derives from a relationship with the Holy Spirit and holds that Scripture has something to say about how modern Christians should view their contemporary culture.

APPLICATION QUESTIONS

1. What warning signs might you recognize if your worldview becomes more influenced by present culture than by Scripture?

2. If the development of a biblical worldview involves allowing the Spirit to cultivate both a mindset and a "willset," how might a radical openness to the Spirit be helpful?

3. Who is a spiritual authority in my life that could guide me toward a biblical worldview? What might happen if I invite them to assist me in my journey toward a more biblical worldview?

FURTHER READING

Dempster, Murray, Byron D. Klaus, and Douglas Petersen, eds. *The Globalization of Pentecostalism: A Religion Made to Travel.* Eugene, OR: Wipf & Stock, 2011.

Smith, James K. A. *Thinking in Tongues: Pentecostal Contributions to Christian Philosophy.* Grand Rapids: Eerdmans, 2010.

Vondey, Wolfgang. *The Routledge Handbook of Pentecostal Theology.* Abingdon, Oxfordshire: Routledge, 2020.

Warrington, Keith. *Pentecostal Theology: A Theology of Encounter.* London: Bloomsbury Academic, 2008.

Welker, Michael. *The Work of the Spirit: Pneumatology and Pentecostalism.* Grand Rapids: Eerdmans, 2006.

2

Perspectives on Scripture

Because the Bible is God's Word, it has eternal relevance; it speaks to all human-kind, in every age and in every culture.

—GORDON FEE

INTRODUCTION

In the fourth book of C. S. Lewis's Chronicles of Narnia series, *The Silver Chair*, Jill Pole speaks with the lion Aslan on a majestic mountain before embarking on a long voyage to locate the missing prince. Aslan gives Jill four signs to remember throughout the journey and informs her that following these signs is the key to fulfilling the reason that Aslan has brought her to Narnia:

> But, first, remember, remember, remember the signs. Say them to yourself when you wake in the morning and when you lie down at night, and when you wake in the middle of the night. And whatever strange things may happen to you, let nothing turn your mind from following the signs. And secondly, I give you a warning. Here on the mountain I have spoken to you clearly: I will not often do so down in Narnia. Here on the mountain, the air is clear and your mind is clear; as you drop down into Narnia, the air will thicken. Take great care that it does not confuse your mind. And the signs which you have learned here will not look at all as you expect them to look, when you meet them there. That is why it is so important to know them by heart and pay no attention to

appearances. Remember the signs and believe the signs. Nothing else matters.[1]

However, despite Aslan's warning, there are times when Jill determines she knows the best way forward and, in her self-assurance, forges her own path instead of heeding the signs provided by Aslan. As you might expect, she falls off the path whenever she attempts to interpret the signals differently than what Aslan had stated. Like Jill, the Christian has been given a sign that God asks us to read and follow, the Word of God.

While many Christians know the Bible consists of many books (sixty-six to be exact), fewer have thought about how their interpretive approach profoundly impacts their reading of Scripture. Biblical hermeneutics is the field of study that examines the method of interpreting Scripture. God has chosen to enable the construction of the Bible to come through human writers. However, these authors did not write driven by their own agenda or purposes, but they were "men moved by the Holy Spirit [who] spoke from God" (2 Pet 1:21). While the divine-human relationship of sacred Scripture is error-free, this does not imply that every "scripturally based" viewpoint should be assumed to be correct. In other words, just because someone uses the Bible to "prove" their view does not mean their interpretation of Scripture is correct. Therefore, interpreting the Word of God requires a willingness to examine whether or not the method used to arrive at a conclusion is "accurately handing the word of truth" (2 Tim 2:15).

"Hermeneutics" may sound intimidating; however, the truth is every human is well versed in using interpretive skills though they may not realize it. In fact, you have been taught hermeneutics all your life and even unconsciously are using these interpretive skills every time you interpret human language.[2] Every time you interact with language, you use hermeneutics to make sense of the words being communicated. This skill is so natural to us that it is only after we discover we have misinterpreted the meaning of something that we are forced to awaken to our potential for hermeneutical error. For example, I grew up in the Midwest, so if someone asked me, "Would you like some iced tea?," my cultural interpretation of that question would lead me to assume that the tea would be unsweetened. However, when I moved to Texas, I quickly learned that if someone asks, "Would you like some iced tea?," the question is culturally interpreted to assume the tea would be sweetened (undisguisable from syrup). How is it that the same

1. Lewis, *The Silver Chair*, 26.

2. Kaiser, Walter C, and Silva Moisés. *Introduction to Biblical Hermeneutics*, 17.

exact question can result in two very different meanings? The answer is quite simple: hermeneutics.

Hermeneutics is the field of study concerned with how we interpret language and it is unavoidable if we hope to discover meaning. However, as the previous illustration reveals, hermeneutical interpretations of human language are prone to misinterpretation. While a misunderstanding over the nature of tea is a minor misreading of meaning, the misinterpretation of Scripture can have eternally significant consequences. This is why it is important that every Christian think through their hermeneutical approach to reading Holy Scripture.

Biblical hermeneutics focuses on examining the process used to interpret the meaning of the Bible and the goal of hermeneutics should be to discover the original author's intended purpose. At this point, it is essential to note every Christian has a biblical hermeneutic, whether they realize it or not. Just like every person uses a method to interpret everyday language, every Christian possesses a biblical hermeneutic for interpreting the meaning of Scripture. The question is not whether the Christian possesses a hermeneutical approach to reading Scripture; the question is whether they have examined their approach carefully. I heard of a man who once complained to Samuel Clemens (best known by his pen name, Mark Twain) that the Bible was all jumbled up, inconsistent, and filled with passages he could not understand. The humorist replied, "I have more difficulty with the passages I do understand than with the passages I do not understand." One of the marvelous truths about Scripture is that no matter where you are in your journey of reading Scripture, it is both understandable and immeasurably deep.

Every orthodox Christian should approach Scripture with a biblical hermeneutic that begins with the assumption that "all Scripture is inspired by God" (2 Tim 3:16). Without this basic assumption, the Bible loses all its divine authority and usefulness for Christian living. Yet, within orthodox Christianity, many theological traditions exist that have various ways of reading and interpreting Scripture. The fact that numerous traditions can all look at the same Bible and yet interpret it very differently should highlight the importance of theological assumptions often brought to interpreting Scripture. While it is impossible to have a hermeneutic free from all presuppositions, the reader of Scripture is wise to recognize that they are susceptible to bringing certain cultural or traditional assumptions to the task of interpreting the Bible. Such cultural or traditional assumptions may or may not be in line with what the original author intended to communicate. The reader of God's Word has a critical responsibility to be honest and humble enough to adjust their beliefs about the interpretation of a text when confronted with evidence that their assumptions were wrong.

To adjust one's interpretation of a certain passage of Scripture does not mean that the Word of God was wrong; it only means that one's interpretation was in error. Unfortunately, some Christians are unwilling to adjust their interpretation of a passage of Scripture even when they agree that there is no evidence for continuing to hold to their false interpretation. When this occurs, a real tragedy takes place, for the study of God's Word stops becoming about discovering the author's intended meaning and becomes about protecting a particular interpretation. For example, most biblical scholars today recognize that cessationism (the belief that the gifts of the Spirit stopped after the apostles) lacks biblical support.[3] However, despite this reality, many Christians still hold to this belief and are unwilling to adjust their cultural or traditional assumptions about spiritual gifts. This is but one example of numerous issues where cultural or traditional interpretations of God's Word can prevent the reader from accepting the original intent of the biblical authors.

Given the current postmodern climate, the interpretative quest for meaning is more important than ever before. Absolute truths and objective moral standards are being thrown aside for pluralistic philosophies and ethical relativism. The modern search for meaning is much like the dispute between Humpty Dumpty and Alice:

> "When I use a word," Humpty Dumpty said, in rather a scornful tone, "it means just what I choose it to mean—neither more nor less."
>
> "The question is," said Alice, "whether you can make words mean so many different things."
>
> "The question is," said Humpty Dumpty, "which is to be master—that is all."
>
> Alice was too much puzzled to say anything.[4]

Much like Alice, our current culture is facing a crisis of meaning. Our postmodern society has embraced the philosophy of Humpty Dumpty and people are trying to become their own god and create their own meaning. In an attempt to upend God's design, our society is seeking to change the

3. Keener, *Spirit Hermeneutics*, 11.

4. Carroll, *Through the Looking Glass*,

meaning of such fundamental words such as "male" and "female." Given our current social climate, the Christian has been given a powerful opportunity to present a relevant biblical hermeneutic of Scripture that will allow God's Word to speak the truth of the gospel (John 14:6; 17:17). However, the only way the Christian can do this effectively is when they interpret the Bible in a posture of honest examination and humble reverence.

APPROACHING SCRIPTURE

The predominant belief of the people of God throughout church history has been that the text of Scripture is both sacred (inspired by the Holy Spirit and thus bearing God's authority) and relevant to contemporary life. Therefore, engaging with Scripture is more than merely an intellectual task, but a dynamic interaction with the Word of life (1 John 1:1).

Holy Scripture is both a divine and human book. Because God chose to speak His word through human words, every book of the Bible is bound to the original author's language, time, and culture. This is a basic fact most readers of the Bible miss. Therefore, interpreting God's Word correctly requires a tension between its eternal relevance and its historical

Holy Scripture is both a divine and human book. Because God chose to speak His word through human words, every book of the Bible is bound to the original author's language, time, and culture.

context.[5] This means the text of Scripture invites us to understand how God revealed Himself within an ancient context. In other words, God's Word did not originate in our present lifetime, in our culture, or in our native language (unless you grew up reading ancient Greek and Hebrew). Therefore, if we are to read and understand Scripture correctly, we must embrace the truth that *every* aspect of Scripture has been communicated within a context that is foreign to our current environment.

This may seem like a basic observation; however, I am constantly amazed about how many American Christians approach the Bible as if it

5. Fee and Stuart, *How to Read the Bible for All It's Worth*, 25.

were a Western, English, twenty-first-century book, when the truth is actually the exact opposite: God communicated Scripture first to an ancient Near Eastern people who spoke a Semitic language and whose culture was dramatically different than ours. This is not to suggest that the Bible has no relevance to our modern culture, for it certainly does. Instead, the point is that every serious student of Scripture must strive to first understand the context in which God first spoke so that the they can apply that same divine message to our present age. To this point, Gordon Fee states,

> Our understanding of the nature of Scripture is that the Bible is God's word spoken in human words in history. As God's word it has eternal relevance; he addresses us. It is ours to hear and obey. But as human words in history the eternal word has historical particularity. None of the words was spoken in a vacuum.[6]

Secular readers of the Bible approach it as though it were nothing more than a book filled with old stories that are no more significant than the writings of other ancient fables written about the gods. On the other hand, many modern Christians view Scripture as *only* a divine book and, therefore, ignore the original author's history, culture, and language. Viewing the Bible only through a divine lens, they quickly forget that before Scripture was God's Word to us today, it was first God's Word to the original audience. This means Scripture has a definite meaning in its historical context and this meaning must be the anchor to our present interpretation.[7]

After committing their life to Christ, the average Christian is handed a Bible and told, "Read this; it's God's Word!" Without being trained on how to approach the reading of this ancient book, they stumble around the sacred text left to their own to make sense of the narratives and instructions. Therefore, it is no wonder that many Christians approach Scripture from a fundamental misunderstanding of how to interpret the Bible. All of this results in the average American churchgoer treating Scripture as something like a divine motivational book designed solely to encourage their spiritual life. They approach Scripture as if it were a series of motivational tweets from God—divine one-liners, straight from heaven, free from any historical, linguistic, or cultural context.

Without question, the Word of God serves as a tremendous encouragement to our present walk with God. We ought to expect to gain spiritual

---

6. Fee, *Gospel and Spirit*, 30.

7. Pinnock, "Work of the Spirit in the Interpretation of Holy Scripture," 241.

insights that are significant to our current life from our scriptural reading. However, the first rule of reading the Bible is to hear the text on its own terms, not ours.[8] This means we correctly hear the word the original audience heard by understanding what was said to them by the author back then and there. Only after we have done this properly can we hear that same word in the here and now.

Imagine a traveler in a foreign country trying to navigate the streets without a map or guide. They might make some progress, but they will likely get lost or miss essential landmarks along the way. But if they have a map and a guide, they can confidently navigate, understanding the context of the land and the culture around them. Similarly, when readers of the Bible fail to think about their hermeneutic, they are likely to get lost in their interpretations and inadvertently misinterpret simply because they have failed to consider the text's historical and cultural context, literary genre, and structure. Just as a traveler with a map and guide can confidently navigate a foreign land, so too can the Christian confidently navigate the Word of God using sound principles of interpretation.

Through the power of the Spirit, the Bible is the primary way God shapes the Christian into the image of Christ. What is more, a distinctively Pentecostal hermeneutic offers a unique interpretive perspective that emphasizes the work of the Spirit in the reading of Scripture. With this understanding, it is critical that the Christian learn to read the Bible with a desire to place it within the specific location and in the original context that the triune God first established it. Only after we have completed this step can we begin to apply those same Spirit-inspired principles to our current situation. Although the Pentecostal hermeneutic is a restorative hermeneutic, that does not mean that it desires to produce a new hermeneutic. As "people of the Spirit," Pentecostals should not seek out new or novel words, but rather be desirous of hearing the Spirit speak the same words to us today that he inspired the first time.

A PENTECOSTAL PERSPECTIVE

Like mainline Christian traditions, a central perspective of classical Pentecostalism is the conviction that "all Scripture is inspired by God" (2 Tim 3:16). This foundational perspective views the Bible as the faithful

---

8. Keener, *Spirit Hermeneutics*, 25.

revelation of God that proclaims the precise truths the Holy Spirit intended to convey to humanity about the person and work of Jesus Christ.

What makes the Pentecostal hermeneutic unique is the way in which the Pentecostal sees themselves in connection to sacred Scripture. For the Pentecostal, the Bible is not simply a historical record of God's working among ancients peoples, but it is a practical invitation to live within the same Spirit-filled community exhibited in Scripture. The Pentecostal reads the Bible as a person who is also living out a biblical experience—not limited in terms of ancient culture—but as a person living by the same Spirit who guided God's people as recorded in God's Word.[9] This means the Pentecostal views the Holy Spirit as the unifying agent who bridges the distance between the ancient context of Scripture and its present application.

According to a Pentecostal hermeneutic, if a biblical truth is going to be transmitted, that truth needs to be able to be experienced in real life. In other words, the Spirit that spoke through the biblical authors desires to speak that same word to the church today in practically applicable ways. This is exactly what the modern Pentecostal revival has sought to convey to the wider church world.[10] As the author of Scripture, the Spirit serves as the common denominator that bridges the temporal and cultural distance between the original author and the modern interpreter.[11] The Pentecostal sees the Spirit as the one who has faithfully guided the church "into all the truth" (John 16:13) and who provides a permanent link that runs between the original author's meaning and its contemporary meaning.

Pentecostal scholar French Arrington points out four unique ways that the Pentecostal views the influence of the Holy Spirit in guiding their reading of Scripture:

> (1) submission of the mind to God so that the critical and analytical abilities are exercised under the guidance of the Holy Spirit, (2) a genuine openness to the witness of the Spirit as the text is examined, (3) the personal experience of faith as part of the entire interpretative process, and (4) response to the transforming call of God's Word.[12]

In other words, the Pentecostal approaches God's Word through: (1) submitting to the Spirit's guidance in the task of studying of God's Word, (2)

---

9. Keener, *Spirit Hermeneutics*, 5.

10. Menzies, "Methodology of Pentecostal Theology," 13.

11. Ramm, *Witness of the Spirit*, 31.

12. Arrington, "Use of the Bible by Pentecostals," 105.

sincerity in looking for the activity of the Spirit in Scripture, (3) integrating their personal faith in the interpretative process, and (4) willingness to response to the Spirit's transformational power found in Scripture.

These fundamental principles underpin a Pentecostal reading of the Bible, which seeks to unify what the Spirit said with what the Spirit is saying today. The Pentecostal church, as an Acts 29 community, views the believer as participating in the same work of the Spirit that was narrated in the New Testament, albeit in a different context and culture. Yet, since we are people of the same Spirit, the motto of the Pentecostal hermeneutical approach is: *We are the post-Pentecost people of God.*[13] Such a perspective allows the Pentecostal to approach God's Word both in light of Pentecost (historical context) and after Pentecost (through church history until present context). Through both perspectives, the Pentecostal can trace the Spirit as the guiding force that illuminates the Word of Life.

The motto of the Pentecostal hermeneutical approach is: *We are the post-Pentecost people of God.*

A Pentecostal hermeneutical approach to the Bible considers the connection between the Holy Spirit—as the animator of Scripture—and His present empowering of the community of faith. It also considers how the Spirit uses God's Word to equip us for ministry and witness in culturally appropriate ways.[14] This means the Pentecostal looks to Scripture as a Spirit-inspired guide for how to be a Spirit-empowered community in our present context. While the cultural environment may differ between the first-century ministry context and our current culture, the Pentecostal looks for principles and guidance from Scripture that can be applied to their present culture. In short, the Pentecostal hermeneutic can be summarized as a "This is that!" hermeneutic.[15]

13. Oliverio Jr., *Pentecostal Hermeneutics*, 66.

14. Nel, "Attempting to Define a Pentecostal hermeneutics," 3.

15. Richie, *Essential of Pentecostal Theology*, 3.

Additionally, the Pentecostal sees the Spirit's activity in God's Word to provide them with confidence that the same Spirit that empowered the witness of the first-century church will also empower their missional efforts. The Pentecostal reads the Bible not merely for devotional encouragement, but for missional inspiration. The missional confidence of the Pentecostal is renewed as they are transformed through an encounter with God in Scripture. As they experience the *missio Spiritus* (mission of the Spirit) within the pages of the Bible, the Pentecostal community is energized and inspired to bear witness to the same power and love of God within our present age. Therefore, the Pentecostal is interested in God's Word not merely for what it teaches about ancient history, but because they expect to share in the same spiritual experience and connection with God that they read about in Scripture.[16]

A Pentecostal perspective on Holy Scripture emphasizes the importance of the historical context and message of the original authors while at the same time desiring to see the same Spirit-inspired message be realized within their current context. The Pentecostal seeks to avoid two errors: (1) missing the historical context and original intent of the author and thereby misinterpret God's Word, and (2) studying Scripture without allowing it to impact their lived experience in the Spirit. Within these two guardrails, the Pentecostal enjoys a dynamic reading of the Bible that is connected to its historical past and our present by the person and work of the Holy Spirit.

CONCLUSION

The modern Christian is wise to appreciate the historical and cultural context of Scripture when interpreting it. Because the Word of God is both a divine and human book, each book of the Bible is bound to the original author's language, time, and culture. As a result, correctly interpreting Scripture requires a connection between its eternal relevance and its historical context. While secular readers of the Bible approach the book as nothing more than a collection of old stories, the Christian believes it is a divinely inspired work. Yet, even though the Bible possesses a divine author, the Christian must appreciate and understand its historical and cultural context. As modern readers of an ancient text, it is important that readers of Scripture approach the text on its own terms, not ours. This

---

16. Keener, *Spirit Hermeneutics*, 5.

means understanding what was said to the original audience and only then applying those same Spirit-inspired principles to our current situation.

The Pentecostal perspective on hermeneutics emphasizes the work of the Spirit in the reading of Scripture. For Pentecostals, the Bible is not simply a historical record of God's working among ancient peoples but is a practical invitation to live within the same Spirit-filled community exhibited in God's Word. Therefore, Pentecostals read the Bible as people who are living out a walk of faith that experiences the same Spirit that guided and empowered the people found within the pages of Scripture.

APPLICATION QUESTIONS

1. How might a careful examination of your approach to reading Scripture improve your experience with God's Word?

2. How does the Spirit serving as the unifying connector between the original authors and the reader help us in our approach to Scripture?

FURTHER READING

Archer, Kenneth. *A Pentecostal Hermeneutic for the Twenty-First Century: Spirit, Scripture and Community*. Londn: A & C Black, 2004.

Fee, Gordon D., and Douglas Stuart. *How to Read the Bible for All Its Worth*. 4th ed. Grand Rapids: Zondervan, 2014.

Keener, Craig S. *Spirit Hermeneutics: Reading Scripture in Light of Pentecost*. Grand Rapids: Eerdmans, 2016.

Mather, Hannah R. K. *The Interpreting Spirit: Spirit, Scripture, and Interpretation in the Renewal Tradition*. Wipf and Stock Publishers, 2020.

Martin, Lee Roy, ed. *Pentecostal Hermeneutics: A Reader*. Leiden: Brill, 2013.

Oliverio, L. William. *Theological Hermeneutics in the Classical Pentecostal Tradition: A Typological Account*. Leiden: Brill, 2012.

Purdy, Harlyn Graydon. *A Distinct Twenty-First Century Pentecostal Hermeneutic*. Eugene, OR: Wipf & Stock, 2015.

Yong, Amos. *The Hermeneutical Spirit: Theological Interpretation and Scriptural Imagination for the 21st Century*. Wipf and Stock Publishers, 2017.

———. *Spirit-Word-Community: Theological Hermeneutics in Trinitarian Perspective*. London: Routledge, 2017.

3

Perspectives on Salvation

The Spirit is eternal and, being omniscient, is available to guide believers as they gaze at God who beckons them to come ever closer to enjoy the benefits of a remarkable salvation with the help of the remarkable Spirit.

—Keith Warrington

INTRODUCTION

An elderly man was sitting in his rocking chair overlooking his vast farmland with his grandson. As the two sat on the front porch talking and enjoying the sunset, the conversation naturally led to farming.

"You know what all this has in common, Son?" the aged farmer asked the young boy as he pointed to fields.

"No, I guess I don't," the boy replied after thinking about the question for a moment.

"Brokenness!" exclaimed the farmer in such a matter-of-fact manner that it surprised the lad.

Before he could ask for an explanation, the experienced farmer said, "You see, Son, the soil breaks to allow for the crop to be planted, the seed breaks and gives birth to the wheat, the sky breaks to pour out the rain, the wheat breaks to make the bread, and the bread breaks to provide us nourishment."

Taken back by this reality, the young lad asked, "What does this mean, Grandpa?"

Adjusting his glasses to look at his grandson, the wise farmer replied, "It means that even though brokenness is inevitable, it can be redeemed for a greater purpose."

Much like the story illustrates, every facet of human experience has one thing in common, brokenness. The results of Adam and Eve's rebellious act against God's command brought about a new reality throughout the entire creation, marked by the experience that "death spread to all men, because all sinned" (Rom 5:12). The account of humanity's fall reveals that God's judgment for sin extended beyond Adam and Eve to include the whole of the natural world (Gen 3:16–19). Once the dust had settled from humanity's tasting of sin, the outcome was nothing less than cosmic death. The consequences of human sin brought about the rupture of a perfect environment between the Creator and creation as "the Lord God sent him out of the garden of Eden" (Gen 3:24). Therefore, humanity's redemption involves restoring God's relation with a broken universe.

There is a push by some within modern Christianity to soften sin and its universal consequences. In an effort to avoid offending the sinner, attempts are made to minimize sin's all-consuming, all-corrupting nature. Undoubtedly, the adversary of our soul has done fewer more devastating things to fallen humanity than persuading them to believe false narratives about sin. However, all attempts to market sin as a minor mistake or a little mess-up does nothing to change sin's utterly devastating power, for "when sin is accomplished it brings forth death" (Jas 1:15).

Once the dust had settled from humanity's tasting of sin, the outcome was nothing less than cosmic death.

For God's ultimate purpose in salvation to be complete requires the renewal of broken humanity, including their ruined environment. As such, a theology of salvation best fits within an already/not yet paradigm. Such a paradigm views the work of salvation as a work in the past, an active work in our present, and a future hope that is yet to come. In short, it is accurate to say, "I have been saved, I am being saved, and I am yet to be saved!"

Through the death and resurrection of Jesus, the redemption of humanity and the restoration of our broken environment has begun. Still, the completion of salvation will not yet be fully realized until the redemption of all creation takes place in new heaven and new earth (Rev 21:1–5). A biblical theology of salvation emphasizes the importance of salvation being both an otherworldly and a this-worldly act, connecting the work of redemption to our present state and our future hope.[1]

PERSPECTIVES ON SALVATION

Next time you are at the airport, notice the difference between passengers who have confirmed tickets and those who are on standby. The ones with confirmed tickets read newspapers, talk with their friends, or busy themselves with work. This is quite different from the way those who are on standby act. Those on standby hang around the ticket counter; they pace and fret, worried about whether or not they will get to their destination. The person on standby is haunted by an internal anxiety about their future. With no confidence or control over their travel, standby is a bad place to be. Worse than standby at an airport, traveling through life without eternal assurance is a horrible existence. This is why the study of salvation (soteriology) is critical, because it helps us understand what the Bible has to say about God's redemptive work in humanity and His eternal plans for those who put their faith in Christ.

Because of sin, humanity is separated from God, making salvation necessary for us to reunite with God. While many other religions propose various methods for attaining enlightenment or improving one's fate in the afterlife, Christianity teaches that humanity is inherently flawed by a sinful nature and only through the death and resurrection of Jesus Christ can forgiveness and reconciliation with God be achieved. Through justification, those who were once out of fellowship with God "have peace with God through our Lord Jesus Christ" (Rom 5:1). Having peace with God is a complete transformation from our previous sinful status in which we continued to rebel against God, "storing up wrath for yourself in the day of wrath" (Rom 2:5). But through Christ's atoning work, the person who places their faith in Jesus can now live in a restored relationship with God.[2]

1. Richie, *Saved, Delivered, and Healed*, 110.

2. Macchia, *Tongues of Fire*, 468.

At this point, it is critical to note that a Pentecostal perspective on the order of salvation differs fundamentally from Catholic and Reformed perspectives. Within a Catholic view of salvation, the sacraments (water baptism, penitence, and the Eucharist) play a critical role in the process of one's redemption from sin. The inherent problem with tying such practices to salvation is that it promotes a works-based salvation.

A friend of mine once made a very generous offer to me. He approached me and stated that he wanted to pay entirely for an upcoming trip I would be taking. He wanted to provide me with flights, hotel rooms, meals, and anything else I might need for the most pleasant trip possible. There was only one condition: if I paid for anything on the trip, I had to pay for everything. In other words, he would pay for the whole trip, or I would owe for everything. Much like the story illustrates, God has offered humanity a means of eternal salvation, but we cannot contribute anything to this eternal trip. God's Word is clear: our salvation is not dependent upon our good works, "for by grace you have been saved through faith; and that not of yourselves, it is the gift of God; not as a result of works, so that no one may boast" (Eph 2:8–9). To this point Pentecostal scholar Hollis Gause writes,

> Any doctrine of salvation by works/merit assumes the inherent goodness of people. It claims that even though there is evidence of some degree of fall in the human race, fallen men and women are able to satisfy the demands of the holy God. Whatever God demands is deemed to be within the creature's ability.[3]

In connecting salvation to the sacramental activities of the church, a Catholic view of salvation links the gospel to human works rather than seeing it as originating solely by faith in Christ's work and God's grace.

Additionally, a Reformed perspective of salvation (Calvinism) teaches that God chooses some people for salvation—the elect, or those people will be saved—while the rest of humanity is predestined for eternal damnation. The Calvinist teaches that God sovereignly chose individuals for salvation before the foundation of the world and those whom God has predestined will eventually come to faith in Christ because God's grace is irresistible.

From a Pentecostal perspective, there are several fundamental errors within the Calvinist view on salvation. First, Calvinism's doctrine of predestination and election limits God's love and mercy to a select few individuals while leaving the rest of humanity eternally damned. This view contradicts

---

3. Richie, *Saved, Delivered, and Healed*, 110.

the biblical teaching that, "God our Savior, who desires all men to be saved" (1 Tim 2:3–4) and that salvation is available to "whoever believes in Him" (John 3:16). Secondly, the Calvinist view of God's sovereignty in salvation promotes a fatalistic view of life and undermines the importance of human free will. Additionally, it suggests that once someone comes to faith in Christ, they can never reject their faith. This notion of "once saved, always saved" is a perspective that goes against scriptural teachings (Gal 5:4; Jas 5:19–20; 2 Peter 2:20–22; Heb 3:12).

Instead, a biblical framework of God's sovereignty does not negate human free will, but rather views God as working in concert with it (John 7:17; Rev 3:20). Since our will is distinct from God's, the Christian must cooperate with divine grace in order for that grace to be realized in our life. Yet the very fact that God has given us free will is in and of itself an act of God's graciousness. Therefore, cooperation with grace itself comes from divine grace.[4] In short, salvation is all a work of God's grace, yet it includes our willingness to cooperate within God's grace.

Finally, the Calvinist view of irresistible grace implies that those who have not been predestined for salvation have no hope of being saved. There-fore, their responsiveness to the gospel is beyond their control. This view contradicts the biblical teaching that salvation is available to all who repent and believe in Christ (Acts 2:38–39; Rom 10:9–13). As a free gift, God has given each person the ability to accept or reject His offer of salvation, and our response to God's grace is an integral part of the process (Matt 16:24; Rom 6:23). In summarizing the Pentecostal perspective, Tony Richie writes,

> Pentecostals are Wesleyan-Arminian because of commitment to the biblical declaration that "Whoever desires" may "take the water of life freely" (Revelation 22:17). In short, Pentecostal's high view of scriptural inspiration and authority is determinative for the shape of Pentecostal theology.[5]

In contrast to a Calvinist perspective on salvation, the Pentecostal seeks to show that while salvation is wholly the work of God, the application of God's saving work and the reception of the Spirit depend on human response. In this way, the Pentecostal confirms the sovereignty of God while still maintaining humanity's need to respond to God's grace.

4. Macchia, *Tongues of Fire*, 488.

5. Ibid, 121.

A PENTECOSTAL PERSPECTIVE

The Pentecostal framework of the fivefold gospel claims that Jesus Christ is the Savior, Sanctifier, Spirit-Baptizer, Healer, and soon-coming King. When looking at the scope of the fivefold gospel, it is evident that the full gospel is soteriological from beginning to end: all elements are potential points on the way to salvation.[6] This suggests that the Pentecostal views the experience of salvation holistically and looks for how the marks of salvation impact the entirety of the Christian.

In examining a Pentecostal perspective on salvation, it is important to recognize its deeply experiential nature. The Pentecostal values the Spirit's work in drawing people to a salvation encounter with Christ. Through the Spirit's infusion of divine life into those who believe, the Christian is saved from their sins through an encounter with the "Spirit of life" (Rom 8:2). Central to this holistic approach to salvation is the Pentecostal understanding that the act of being born again involves more than just preparation for the afterlife, but it also includes a transformational deliverance within this present age. This includes emotional and physical deliverance from oppressive spirits and spiritual victory that affects the whole of the Christian's life.[7]

Such a perspective of the new birth causes the Pentecostal to expect salvation to bring a radical change in the new believer's life because "the old things passed away; behold new things have come" (2 Cor 5:17). The Pentecostal views salvation much like the radical transformation that takes place in the life of a caterpillar. The caterpillar begins its life crawling along the ground, inching its way through life. But one day the caterpillar enters a cocoon and undergoes a life-changing transformation. The caterpillar dies in its old form and becomes a brand-new creature: a butterfly. Similarly, Pentecostals expect salvation to result in a metamorphosis of nature, resulting in a changed life that is evident to everyone. This transformation of the butterfly is more than an internal feeling, but it is a complete change of nature. Beyond mere theological theory; the Pentecostal insists that all theology be alive in its practical application. Nowhere is this better seen than in a Pentecostal understanding of soteriology. A Pentecostal perspective on the specifics of salvation (faith, repentance, justification, redemption, adoption, sanctification, and assurance) sees it all through an experiential framework. As a result, the Pentecostal salvific experience is

6. Vondey, "Soteriology at the Altar," 223.

7. Richie, *Saved, Delivered, and Healed*, 115.

highly transformational. Central to a Pentecostal understanding of salvation is a relationship with Jesus through an encounter with the Spirit that is expected to change a person in radical ways.

This soteriological emphasis on divine relationship enables the Pentecostal to view salvation as more than a "get out of hell" card or as escapism from present troubles. While repentance includes "godly sorrow" (2 Cor 7:10), it does not let one wallow in never-ending guilt. Instead, the Christian is called to confidently "draw near to the throne of grace" (Heb 4:16) to experience greater heights of freedom in divine relationship as they cling to grace. Motivated by divine relationship, the Pentecostal's theology concerning salvation is closely connected to their end-time hope (more on this in chapter 12).

> **Central to a Pentecostal understanding of salvation is a relationship with Jesus through an encounter with the Spirit that is expected to change a person in radical ways.**

Through the Spirit, the Christian is both reborn and embraced in a divine relationship. This divine embrace allows the believer to enter into fellowship with Christ and His favor with the Father. While we enjoy the benefits of this divine relationship and the freedom that comes from being rescued "from this present evil age" (Gal 1:4), Pentecostal soteriology also emphasizes the Christian's salvific future "so that in the ages to come He might show the surpassing riches of His grace" (Eph 2:7).[8] Through the act of speaking in tongues the Pentecostal provides a small glimpse into our salvific future. As prayer and praise that transcends our human limitations of language, speaking in tongues communicates a longing for the time when our salvation will be complete and where humanity "from every nation and all tribes and peoples and tongues, standing before the throne and before the Lamb, clothed in white robes, and palm branches were in their hands; and they cry out with a loud voice, saying, 'Salvation to our God who sits on the throne, and to the Lamb.'" (Rev 7:9–10). In this way, when Pentecostals practice speaking in tongues, they are practicing their salvific hope.

---

8. Macchia, *Justified in the Spirit*, 294.

Additionally, when the Pentecostal "groans" in tongues (Rom 8:26), they are mourning the reality that this world is not as it should be. Devastated by sin's ruin, all creation longs for new creation. Through speaking in tongues, the Pentecostal practices a continual reminder that it is good to mourn the destruction caused by sin and to echo the cry of all creation for new creation. Through speaking in tongues, the Pentecostal has a unique lens through which to view God's work of salvation. In tongue speech, the Pentecostal can express their theology of salvation: joy and mourning, hope and brokenness. Though we groan now, we will soon be glorified (1 Cor 15:42–58). Though we see dimly now, we will soon see clearly (1 Cor 13:12). Though we wait patiently now, we will soon reap an eternal harvest (Jas 5:7–8).

CONCLUSION

The Pentecostal view of salvation emphasizes its experiential nature and transformative power. Pentecostals see the new birth as redeeming the Christian from their transgressions resulting in emotional, physical, and spiritual deliverance. Through an encounter with the Holy Spirit in the present age, salvation involves a profound transformation in the life of the new believer.

By rejecting the works-based salvation of Catholicism and the "once saved, always saved" Calvinist position on salvation, the Pentecostal perspective emphasizes the importance of human free will and cooperation with divine grace. While salvation is wholly the work of God, the acceptance of God's saving work and the reception of the Spirit depend on human response.

Pentecostals communicate their salvation theology—joy, sadness, hope, and brokenness—in tongues. Through speaking in tongues, the Pentecostal groans for a future state where the only scars of sin's effects will be found in our Redeemer's body. The hope of this glorified state motivates the Pentecostal to continue to obey their Savior with joy and to give their entire lives and allegiance in humble service.

APPLICATION QUESTIONS

1. What are some errors in a Calvinistic perspective on salvation?

2. If Pentecostal theology is a living theology, how might that apply to living out our salvation?

FURTHER READING

Gause, R. Hollis. *Living in the Spirit: The Way of Salvation.* Cleveland, TN: CPT, 2009.

Hart, Larry D. *Truth Aflame: Theology for the Church in Renewal.* Grand Rapids: Zondervan Academic, 2010.

Macchia, Frank D. *Justified in the Spirit: Creation, Redemption, and the Triune God,* Grand Rapids: Eerdmans, 2010.

Richie, Tony. *Saved, Delivered, and Healed: Introducing a Pentecostal Theology of Salvation,* Eugene, OR: Wipf & Stock, 2022.

Studebaker, Steven M. *The Spirit of Atonement: Pentecostal Contributions and Challenges to the Christian Traditions.* London: Bloomsbury, 2021.

4

Perspectives on Discipleship

The Spirit is that divine person whose movement within the heart begins to reorder affective movements and so alter a person's habits of mind.

—DALE M. COULTER

INTRODUCTION

Born in 1938 on the beautiful island of Puerto Rico, Nicky's life was anything but a tropical paradise. His parents, steeped in the dark world of witchcraft and the occult, abused him and discarded him like trash. Feeling angry from this oppressive rejection, Nicky Cruz began to lead a life of rebellion, anger, and violence.

At just fifteen years old, Nicky began looking for a way out and sought refuge in the concrete jungle of New York City. Yet, instead of the paradise he envisioned, he found himself caught up in the clutches of the notorious street gang the Mau Maus. He quickly became comfortable navigating a life of crime and worked his way up to become their leader; his heart continued to harden like the cold, darkened streets he ruled.

However, his life began to take a dramatic turn when he met a street preacher named David Wilkerson. Wilkerson had moved to New York City with a calling to minister to street gangs. One day, Wilkerson approached Cruz and told him that Jesus loved him. In response, Cruz threatened to kill Wilkerson, but Wilkerson continued to share the love of God and the gospel message of hope with Nicky. After several conversations with Wilkerson, the light of Christ eventually broke through Cruz's hardened heart. Nicky accepted Christ as his Savior and abandoned his criminal lifestyle to follow Christ. Cruz's radical transformation even caused him to minister to other gang members and troubled youth. He has since written several biographies and traveled the globe sharing his testimony and spreading the message of the gospel and the power of becoming a disciple of Christ.

The story of Nicky Cruz's accepting of Christ is a powerful testimony of radical transformation. And while not everyone comes from the same depths of evil and wickedness as Nicky did, every sinner who gives their life to Christ ought to experience a radical transformation as they "proclaim the excellencies of Him who has called you out of darkness into His marvelous light" (1 Pet 2:9). Yet, the modern perception of what it means to be a disciple of Jesus is often so far from a biblical perspective. Many think the invitation to follow Christ sounds like the following conversation:

> "Hey, overall good person, would you identify yourself with Me one day a week in a special building?" Jesus asks.
>
> While you ponder this, Jesus goes on to tell you, "Also, don't worry about living like I lived or changing your lifestyle to be like mine."
>
> With your interest now peaked, Jesus makes one final plea. Like a used car salesman giving you their best offer, Jesus says, "OK, all I need for you to do is say you believe in me, and if you do, I promise not take too much of your time or effort."

The modern church has enabled the growth of this thinking by courting customers instead of converts. The contemporary gospel presentation is an invitation to add Jesus to *your* life instead of the biblical picture expressed by Christ, who stated, "If anyone wishes to come after Me, he must deny himself, and take up his cross and follow Me" (Matt 16:24). The invitation from the modern church has shifted from a call to come as you are and be changed by Christ, to simply an invitation to come as you are.

In contrast to modern sensibilities, the concept of discipleship would not have been a foreign idea to those who followed Jesus. Within a first-century context, disciples were students that had already proven their capability to function as a spiritual leader themselves. They would be chosen by rabbis to learn from them directly, following them (even living with them) for several years to learn and develop a lifestyle that mimicked the rabbi.

The New Testament account of Jesus' disciples shows them functioning very much the same.[1]

It is my observation that the modern Christian is suffering from an insufficient understanding of the question, what does it mean to be a disciple of Christian? Even worse, their lack of understanding of the question has led them to a faulty sense of believing that they have the answer, when in fact they do not even biblically understand the question. This problem reaches to the core of many of the problems that can be observed within the modern evangelical community. How is it that the gospel has become so distorted by false gospels? Why is it that many "Christians" are supporting pop-culture philosophies denounced in Scripture? How can it be that the lives of the Christian and non-Christian have increasingly become indistinguishable? How is it that we have more preaching/teaching at our disposal than ever before, yet it has not translated to a more mature church? I believe that the answer to all these issues can be found in the failure of the modern Christian to accurately understand this fundamental question, what does it means to be a disciple of Christ? For to embrace a biblical perspective on what it means to be a disciple of Christ would naturally solve many of these issues.

WHAT IS A CHRISTIAN DISCIPLE?

Some wrongly assert that there are two classes of saved people: Christians and disciples. This popular heresy teaches that a Christian is someone who by faith accepts Jesus as Savior, receives eternal life, and is a part of the family of God, but does nothing more; while a disciple is a more committed Christian who is seriously active in the practice of spiritual disciplines and involved in evangelizing and training others to be followers of Christ. However, there is absolutely no biblical evidence for such a distinction.[2]

Instead, to identify as a disciple of Christ from a New Testament perspective is to choose to embrace a life of suffering and shame in an ungodly world. From the very beginning of the early church, it was obvious to the followers of Christ that to bear the name of Christ meant to be one who suffered for his name. In fact, the early church viewed the endurance of suffering for the name of Christ as *the* genuine sign of loyalty to Christ.[3]

1. Willard, "Discipleship," 236.

2. Hull, *Complete Book of Discipleship*, 34.

3. See Acts 5:41; Rom 5:3; 2 Cor 12:10; Phil 1:29; Col 1:11; 2 Tim 3:12; Heb 10:34; Jas 1:2; 1 Pet 2:13

The inherent persecution and suffering associated with being a disciple of Christ underscores the reality that to be a Christian within a New Testament context meant more than simply agreeing with Christ's teaching or moral philosophies, but involved a call to live like Him.[4] Thus, to be identified as a disciple of Christ, included a willingness to surrender all as a result of bearing his name. A cost which Jesus knew many will deem too high of a price to pay given that "many of His disciples withdrew and were not walking with Him anymore" (John 6:66).

Not only did the idea of being a disciple of Christ ensure a measure of suffering for his name, but it meant the embracing of a completely new identity: "if anyone is in Christ, he is a new creature" (2 Cor 5:17). This new identity in Christ both supersedes all previous forms of identity, "for you are all one in Christ Jesus" (Gal 3:28), and calls the Christian to live contrary to the world around them in dramatic ways, proclaiming "the excellencies of Him who has called you out of darkness into His marvelous light" (1 Pet 2:9). As such, it is not surprising to find that the Acts of the Apostles is one story after another of disciples of Christ being persecuted for their radical identity in Christ.

The evangelical church is standing at a point where a vast majority of churchgoers have lost the profound depths of what it means to be a disciple of Christ. It is as if a fog has descended over Western Christianity, obscuring the path of true discipleship, leaving a generation of people who believe they are on the way that is "narrow that leads to life" (Matt 7:14) while they continue to walk in a lifestyle that is devoid of biblical discipleship. Some naively assume that following Jesus is primarily about going to church or keeping a set of moral codes. Countless others tragically believe that to be a follower of Christ is all about getting a better life and finding happiness and success. In short, the modern philosophy about being a follower of Christ comes down to trying to discover Jesus hacks that will improve their journey through life. This is a complete inversion of biblical discipleship.

This continual misunderstanding of what it means to be a Christian disciple has resulted in an entire generation of modern Christians who have no idea what it means to live *in* Christ.[5] The gradual drifting away from a biblical understanding of Christian discipleship has resulted in modern-day Christians struggling with a complete identity crisis. How is it that that which was so clear to the early church has become so foreign to

4. See Eph 5:1–2; Phil 2:5–11; 1 John 2:6; 1 Pet 2:21.

5. 2 Cor 5:17; Gal 2:20; Rom 6:1–14; 8:1.

the modern church's sensibilities? How is it that the contemporary church is controlled more by cultural influences than by the culture of the kingdom of heaven? Why is it the average Christian is incapable of enduring suffering for Christ? The answer to these (and many more) issues facing the modern church will only come when we biblically answer the question, what does it mean to be a disciple of Christ? The writers of Holy Scripture offer two analogies that answer this critical question, an alien and a slave.

ALIENS AND SLAVES

For many, the first thing that comes to mind when you hear the word "alien" is a short grayish extraterrestrial with an elongated head and large eyes that rides in a flying saucer. However, whenever the Bible uses this term, it does so in the more traditional meaning of the word, referring to a resident of a foreign land. According to the apostle Peter, the church is an assembling of "aliens and strangers" (1 Pet 2:11). This collection of aliens is making a pilgrimage through this present world anticipating the fullness of the kingdom of heaven to be accomplished. This concept stretches throughout Scripture; from Abraham leaving Ur and the exodus of Israel out of Egypt, to the New Testament authors, the theme of God's people being aliens is common. Sometimes it is in just a few words (as in 1 Peter) and other times the idea is woven through a whole epistle (Hebrews).[6] What is evident is that the first disciples of Christ believed their task of following Jesus centered around embracing the identity of an alien.

While the practical outworking of this perspective is varied, at minimum, it means the disciple of Christ has a distinct identity that separates them from those who are not disciples of Christ. As aliens in this world, the Christian disciple embraces a lifestyle foreign to the person who has not committed their life to Christ. There is something tragically wrong when the unbeliever observes the life of the Christian and does not scratch their head in bewilderment. This does not mean the disciple of Christ's goal is to live a weird lifestyle simply for the shock value of being odd. The objective is not to be weird; the objective is to be Christlike. However, the call of the people of God to be holy (separate, distinct, or other) will result in the disciple of Christ separating themselves from the evil passions of this world and living in a way that pleases God (1 Pet 1:14–17), which by its very nature will be bizarre to the person who is not a disciple of Christ.

6. Dunning, *Aliens and Sojourners*, 46.

Additionally, the overwhelmingly consistent way the first disciples of Christ self-identify in their relationship to Christ is as a slave.[7] Given our modern perspective, the term "slave" is one we intensely dislike (and rightfully so). While Israel—like all ancient Near Eastern people—took slavery for granted as an unalterable fact of life, the humanization of slavery within Israel comes from God constantly reminding them of their own history as slaves (Deut 5:15; 15:15; Lev 25:25).

Since the Israelites came from Egypt as slaves, they were intimately aware of the suffering associated with a hard taskmaster Therefore, in comparison to other ancient Near Eastern societies, Israel's laws concerning slaves were much more humane. For example, Jewish slaves had to be released after six years, unless they chose to remain as slaves. The only exception for the Jewish slaves was for the slave that chose to remain with their master at the end of the six years of servitude, whose ear would then be pierced. But if the slave decided to leave their master after six years of servitude, their master was required to give them provisions that would enable them to become self-sufficient (Ex 21:5–6; Deut 15:12–17).

Yet, the central issue of slavery is the total dependence of the slave upon the master. Whether ancient or modern, slavery implies the surrender of freedom and the reality of belonging wholly to another. Therefore, an enslaved person (literal or figurative) is someone whose whole person and service belong entirely to another. Simply put, slavery involves absolute ownership and control on the part of the master and the total subjection of the slave.[8] It is exactly this New Testament picture that the disciples continually use to describe their connection to Jesus Christ.

Given the fact the New Testament disciples viewed themselves as slaves of Christ, the question must be asked, where did they get this idea? This perspective did not originate with the apostles. Instead, the followers of Christ took on the example of their Master, who "emptied Himself, taking the form of a bond-servant" (Phil 2:7) to set humanity free from their previous condition as "slaves to sin" (Rom 6:20). Therefore, it was a transformational encounter with the resurrected Christ and the indwelling of the Spirit upon them that moved them to adopt a radically new perspective. It is this same Spirit-inspired encounter with the living Christ that motivates the modern disciple of Christ to have the same identity as the first disciples.

7. Rom 1:1; Phil 1:1; Titus 1:1; Jas 1:1; 2 Pet 1:1; Jude 1:1.

8. Harris, *Slave of Christ*, 26.

To embrace the identity of an alien in this world and a slave to Christ is a far cry from the contemporary perspective on discipleship. Many modern followers of Jesus believe becoming Christ's disciple is all about Jesus blessing their efforts and plans. Countless contemporary disciples wrongly assume that being Jesus' disciple is about getting a cosmic genie who will assist them in fulfilling their material goals. They think the gospel of Christ is designed to bring them health, wealth, and prosperity. In short, many within Western Christianity have allowed Christian discipleship to be hijacked by the American dream, resulting in biblical discipleship becoming wholly inverted from being Christ-centered to becoming self-centered. Such an upending of the biblical perspective cannot help but have a devastating impact on one's understanding the Christian life.

A PENTECOSTAL PERSPECTIVE

The central focus of Pentecostal spirituality is an active encounter with the Spirit. Thus, the starting place for thinking about Pentecostal discipleship is life in the Spirit of God and not simply knowledge about God. The Pentecostal desires for their beliefs and behaviors to be guided and influenced by the Spirit. Therefore, the Pentecostal invites the

In short, many within Western Christianity have allowed Christian discipleship to be hijacked by the American dream, resulting in biblical discipleship becoming wholly inverted from being Christ-centered to becoming self-centered.

Spirit of the whole gospel to alter and control the whole person in radical ways.[9] The Pentecostal believes their eagerness to explore the limitlessness of the Spirit's empowerment to be the driving force of their discipleship and spiritual formation.

One of the central roles of the Spirit is to point humanity toward Christ (John 15:26). The Pentecostal sees the Spirit as the empowering force in the Christian life that brings about a renovation of our human nature. By conforming us to the image of Christ, the Spirit guides and motivates Christian

9. Coulter, "Whole Gospel for the Whole Person," 161.

discipleship (2 Cor 3:18; Rom 8:29; Col 3:10). Since the Spirit inspires the Christian toward Christlike living, a Pentecostal perspective on discipleship welcomes the Spirit to keep discipleship Christ-centered.

In 1908 the *Apostolic Faith* (a newspaper published by the Azusa Street Mission) admonished Pentecostals to surrender their lives to Christ fully by forsaking unholy passions and living after the Spirit:

> This Gospel means a crucified life. We must take up our cross daily and follow Christ. The cause of so many losing the anointing of the Spirit is that they neglect to mortify and crucify self. He wants our eyes, our ears, and all our members kept holy unto Him, that we might live after the Spirit and not after the flesh. He is looking for a people today that will die out to the flesh. How can our eyes revel in the things of the world and our ears listen to worldly music if they are consecrated to the Master's use. People say this is fanaticism, but it is the teaching of the precious word of God. We must measure up to it. He wants us to have our ears closed to the world and open to heaven.[10]

From the very beginning of Pentecostalism it is evident that they viewed Christian discipleship as requiring the abandonment of worldly passions in pursuit of a Spirit-directed life. It is the empowerment of the Spirit that motivates and guides the Christ-centered disciple to embrace the radical posture of aliens in this world and slaves of Christ. If a biblical perspective on Christian discipleship centers on embracing the identity of an alien and a slave, then a Pentecostal perspective emphasizes the necessity of the Spirit in aiding this lifestyle. It could be said that the Pentecostal views themselves as a Spirit-empowered alien and a Spirit-empowered slave. In short, the Pentecostal would highlight the indispensable aid of Spirit-empowerment in facilitating their quest of being an alien in this world and the slave of Christ.

Recognizing the inherent human weaknesses involved in trying to be the disciple of Christ, the Pentecostal would express their utter dependency on the Spirit to assist them in living as a Spirit-empowered alien and a Spirit-empowered slave. But with Spirit-inspired confidence, the Pentecostal boldly adopts this way of living, knowing that the Spirit will help them in conforming their life to the image of Christ. This Spirit-inspired confidence shapes Pentecostal discipleship and enables them to boldly stand up against ungodly culture and wicked philosophies of men (Gal 1:10; Rom 12:2; 2

---

10. *The Apostolic Faith*, January 1908, 3.

Cor 10:1–5). Identifying as a Spirit-empowered alien and slave provides the Pentecostal disciple courage and purpose as they live to serve another Master whose "kingdom is not of this world" (John 18:36).

It is not an accident that classical Pentecostalism has historically emphasized the importance of Spirit baptism. The Pentecostal sees a direct connection between Spirit baptism and their living as a disciple of Christ. Having embraced the lifestyle of a Spirit-empowered alien and slave, the Pentecostal believes Spirit baptism is indispensable to their spiritual life. As such, a Pentecostal perspective on discipleship understands Spirit baptism as a driving force in their willingness to abandon earthly comforts and submit to their Master's commands.

CONCLUSION

A biblical perspective on Christian discipleship reveals that the follower of Christ is someone who has chosen to live a life of humble servanthood in this godless world. Being a Christian disciple involves more than simply believing Christ's teachings or moral philosophies; it must include a commitment to live as He did. It entails adopting a brand-new identity in Christ that supersedes all previous identities, as well as living in a way that proclaims the glory of our Redeemer. Also, the Christian disciple is commanded to adopt a lifestyle that is foreign to those who are not saved. They are called to separate themselves from the evil passions of this world in order to live in a manner that is pleasing to God. The repeated analogies used by the biblical authors to describe this way of Christian living are: an alien and a slave.

> **Recognizing the inherent human weaknesses involved in trying to be the disciple of Christ, the Pentecostal would express their utter dependency on the Spirit to aid them in living as a Spirit-empowered alien and a Spirit-empowered slave.**

Throughout its historical development, classical Pentecostalism has emphasized the vital significance of Spirit baptism. This is no mere coincidence. The Pentecostal believer senses a direct correlation between Spirit baptism and their pursuit of authentic discipleship in Christ. Adopting the lifestyle of a Spirit-empowered foreigner in this world and a Spirit-empowered servant of Christ, the Pentecostal embraces Spirit baptism as a crucial and transformative aspect of their spiritual journey. From this perspective, Spirit baptism becomes the catalyst for their willingness to abandon worldly comforts and submit wholeheartedly to their Master's commands.

APPLICATION QUESTIONS

1. Does Scripture intend that every follower of Christ identify as an alien of this world and a slave of Christ, or only special Christians?

2. What might change in your discipleship journey by viewing yourself as a Spirit-empowered alien and slave?

FURTHER READING

Cartledge, Mark J. *The Mediation of the Spirit: Interventions in Practical Theology.* Pentecostal Manifestos. Grand Rapids: Eerdmans, 2015.

Chan, Simon. *Pentecostal Theology and the Christian Spiritual Tradition.* London: A&C Black, 2000.

Coulter, Dale M., and Amos Yong, eds. *The Spirit, the Affections, and the Christian Tradition.* Notre Dame, IN: University of Notre Dame Press, 2016.

Land, Steven Jack. *Pentecostal Spirituality: A Passion for the Kingdom.* London: A&C Black, 1993.

Trementozzi, David. *Salvation in the Flesh: Understanding How Embodiment Shapes Christian Faith.* Eugene, OR: Wipf & Stock, 2018.

5

Perspectives on Spirit Baptism

Pentecostal Christians wholeheartedly believe in the possibility of receiving the same experience of the Holy Spirit today as did the disciples on the Day of Pentecost.

—Tony Richie

INTRODUCTION

Infomercials are painful to watch. The bad acting and the overblown excitement about how this product will change your life is enough to make us roll our eyes. But something is fascinating about how infomercials try to draw us in by promising us more than we excepted. No doubt you have heard the famous line, "But wait, there's more!" What is it about that statement that stirs our interest? There is something powerfully enticing about emphasizing the availability of more.

Pentecostals have traditionally understood Spirit baptism to be the arrival of the Holy Spirit into the believer's life for a specific purpose.[1] Using the Bible as our guide for faith and practice, we should desire all the Spirit has revealed is available to us. However, some Christians hold to a cessationist belief concerning the work of the Spirit. Cessationism teaches that the spiritual gifts outlined in Scripture are no longer in operation within the church and are no longer needed. The cessationist believes there is no such thing as an additional work of the Spirit after conversion. They view

---

1. Horton, *Perspectives on Spirit Baptism*, 47.

the work of the Spirit on the day of Pentecost as the disciple's salvation experience. However, this position originates from a faulty premise that the church was born on the day of Pentecost. A closer examination of God's Word reveals that the church began much earlier than the events depicted in Acts 2.

After Jesus' resurrection, He appeared to the disciples, who were hiding behind closed doors out of fear. Following a greeting of peace, Christ breathed on them and commanded them to "Receive the Holy Spirit" (John 20:22). Since Christ was already crucified, risen, and glorified, the regenerative life of the Spirit—made possible through faith in Christ—could now be administered to Christ's disciples. Thus, we find a redemptive work of the Spirit that precedes the disciple's Spirit baptism on the day of Pentecost.

At Pentecost, those promised to be baptized in the Spirit were said to have been "filled with the Spirit" (Acts 2:4). When recounting his experience to those in Cornelius' house, Peter exchanged the phrase "baptized with the Spirit" for "gift of the Spirit" and then the "Spirit came on us" (Acts 11:15–17).[2] These synonymous terms about Spirit baptism are relevant to our present-day understanding because they make explicit reference to the continued charismatic work of the Spirit.

Luke's narrative within Acts reveals a distinct work of the Spirit that takes place after salvation (Acts 2, 8, 10, 19). The fact that the disciples participated in an additional act of the Spirit on the day of Pentecost does nothing to lessen the first work of the Spirit at salvation. Instead, Spirit baptism facilitates more of the Spirit's work in the believer's life and not a minimizing of his other actions within humanity.

WHY A SIGN?

The actions of the Spirit within humanity occur in ways that are physically observable to us. God has designed His activities within creation to be discernable through our human experience. The divine revelation of creation, Holy Scripture, and the person of Jesus Christ shows the consistent pattern that God wants humanity to be able to identify His works (Ps 19:1; 2 Tim 3:16; John 1:14). While the working of the Spirit is varied; He draws people to salvation (John 16:7–11), produces fruit (Gal 5:22–23), and gives gifts to the church (Eph 4:7–13; 1 Cor 12; Rom 12). The Bible reveals that the workings of the Spirit are manifested in physically observable ways.

2. Hunter, *Spirit Baptism*, 89.

Therefore, any attempt to strip an externally visible sign from Spirit baptism is to miss a significant factor in Scripture's description of the God's action within humanity.

The biblical account presents speaking in tongues as the repeated sign of baptism in the Holy Spirit (Acts 2; 8; 10; 19). It is apparent Luke wanted his readers to understand that Spirit baptism was available to—and indeed should be experienced by—every believer. Throughout the Acts of the Apostles, believers filled with the Spirit spoke in tongues. While the purpose of Spirit baptism is about more than speaking in tongues, as the outward visible sign of Spirit baptism, speaking in tongues remains a critical manifestation of the Spirit's work in our world.[3] Speaking in tongues (Spirit-inspired utterances) serves as the initial (first, but not only) observable (physical) evidence (repeated Biblical marker) of Spirit baptism.

As such, speaking in tongues is like a signpost that points to the Spirit's activity in our lives. If we remove the signpost, we risk missing all it represents. The physical symbol of the wedding ring points to the union of marriage, which has a far deeper significance than a mere circular band. Similarly, the sign of speaking in tongues points to a work of the Spirit that is far more significant than the utterances themselves. Jesus promised that his followers would be "clothed with power from on high" (Luke 24:49).

Some have backed away from supporting speaking in tongues as initial physical evidence of Spirit baptism out of fear that such a position creates a division of Christian classes. However, Spirit baptism is not about making those who speak in tongues better than Christians who have never spoken in tongues. Spirit baptism does not make one more saved or better than the one who is not Spirit baptized. Instead, the emphasis is not about comparing the one who is Spirit baptized against the one who is not; the point is that Spirit baptism makes the one who

> **Speaking in tongues (Spirit-inspired utterances) serves as the initial (first, but not only) observable (physical) evidence (repeated Biblical marker) of Spirit baptism.**

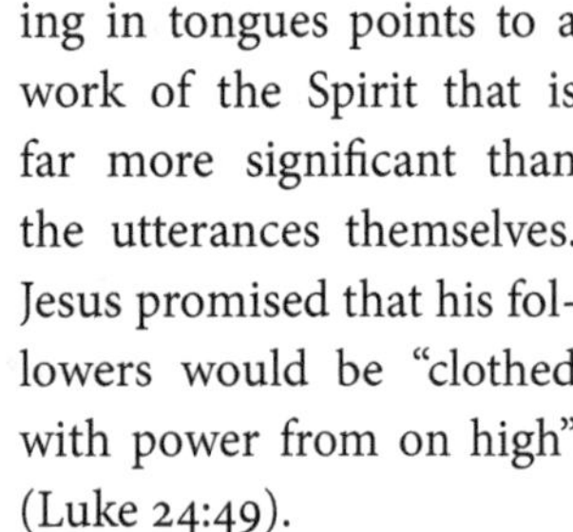

---

3. Laurito, *Speaking in Tongues*, 34.

is baptized "better" by missionally equipping them with "power from on high" (Acts 1:8). In other words, initial physical evidence of Spirit baptism does not create a problem of classification between Christians, but as pictured in the Acts of the Apostles, speaking in tongues empowers the church to be united in mission and equipped for service.

Luke does not present speaking in tongues as evidence of Spirit baptism randomly, but it serves as a supernatural connection between human recipients and Spirit empowerment. At its core, speaking in tongues encompasses an encounter with a divine person whose purpose for sending the Spirit is to transform humanity into His missional partners in advancing God's kingdom "even to the remotest part of the earth" (Acts 1:8).

The classical Pentecostal position on speaking of tongues—as the initial physical evidence of Spirit baptism—is not a marker indicating we are in possession of the Spirit but that the Spirit is in possession of us.[4] This means evidential tongues are not the primary purpose of Spirit baptism. To say speaking in tongues is more than the sign of Spirit baptism is in no way to minimize the significance of evidential tongues as a physical signpost. Instead, it is meant to help us realize that to remove the signpost of evidential tongues damages more than merely a signpost; it risks missing all the signpost is pointing towards. Just as the physical symbolism of water baptism and communion are signposts that point to things much greater than the symbol themselves, evidential tongues point to a work of the Spirit much greater than tongues. Speaking in tongues is not a passive symbol of Spirit baptism but includes the active pursuit of a spiritual life.[5]

> **The classical Pentecostal position of speaking in tongues—as the initial physical evidence of Spirit baptism—is not a marker indicating we are in possession of the Spirit but that the Spirit is in possession of us.**

---

4. Macchia, "Question of Tongues as Initial Evidence," 121.

5. Chan, *Pentecostal Theology*, 72.

A PENTECOSTAL PERSPECTIVE

Before addressing a Pentecostal perspective of Spirit baptism, it is critical to make clear that baptism in the Spirit is not a shortcut to spiritual maturity or a substitute for Christian discipleship. Spirit baptism does not magically remove the continual pursuit of a sanctified life or elevate one to some super-spiritual level. Spirit baptism does not supersede the necessity of the Christian to produce the fruit of the Spirit or to seek the gifts of the Spirit. Instead, the primary purpose of Spirit baptism is the facilitation of Spirit empowerment for missional service and guidance into truth.[6]

The Pentecostal agrees with Jesus' assessment regarding their need for supernatural aid in their missional task (Luke 24:49; Acts 1:8). This posture of utter dependency upon the Spirit to empower their witness motivates the Pentecostal to seek Spirit baptism. It also causes the Pentecostal to see Spirit baptism as central to their radical openness to the "Spirit of truth," who provides illuminating and revelatory guidance (John 16:13). Through initiating, directing, and empowering their missional efforts, Spirit baptism is seen by the Pentecostal as indispensable to their task of being an end-time prophetic voice.

Like the first-century disciples, Pentecostals depend on Spirit empowerment to fulfill the Great Commission and declare the "wonders of God" to the nations (Acts 2:11). Because of this, Pentecostals have traditionally sought a reviving of the Spirit that brings about the same power and experience that marked the early church. This is at the heart of why Pentecostals describe Spirit baptism as an experience distinct from conversion that unleashes a new dimension of the Spirit's power.[7] Pentecostal scholar Wolfgang Vondey explains,

> At the baptism in the Spirit, the holiness of God fills and overflows the receptive capacity of the believer and the community: the praying for the Spirit becomes a praying in the Spirit, the hearing of the gospel becomes a proclamation of the gospel, the laying on of hands becomes an endowment with the Holy Spirit. Such transformations are a consequence of the empowerment with the Spirit.[8]

If the Spirit baptism at Pentecost resulted in the world's evangelization in that day, modern-day Spirit baptism is necessary for the evangelization

6. Richie, *Essentials of Pentecostal Theology*, 183.

7. Macchia, *Baptized in the Spirit*, 20.

8. Vondey, *Pentecostal Theology*, 103.

of our world today. From a Pentecostal perspective, the day of Pentecost was not the day the church began but rather the day the church was empowered. Spirit baptism is about the church receiving Spirit empowerment for missional purposes. Spirit baptism is an empowering calling and gifting that brings life to the witness to Jesus. Therefore, it is the birthright of every Christian as a bearer of the Spirit, "For the promise is for you and your children and for all who are far off, as many as the Lord our God will call to Himself" (Acts 2:39). Given its necessity for missional effectiveness, the Pentecostal views Spirit baptism as essential for every believer to seek.[9]

I will never forget the response of a young man in our church upon receiving the baptism in the Holy Spirit with the evidence of speaking in tongues. I had previously spent many hours talking with him about Spirit baptism and answering his questions about speaking in tongues. But at that moment, he had only one more question. Looking up at me with a broad smile and a face wet with tears, he asked, "Why didn't you tell me it would be this wonderful?" When Pentecostals experience Spirit baptism (as evidenced by speaking in tongues), they are moved with spiritual power that invokes a response. As the human spirit is illuminated by this theophany (a physical manifestation of divine presence) consisting of both divine and human speech, the spiritual life of the believer is moved toward the mission of the Spirit. Not only this, but it is through the continued practice of speaking in tongues that the believer who is baptized in the Spirit is strengthened toward missional effectiveness as they pray or praise in the Spirit.

For the Pentecostal, Spirit baptism is much more than a one-time event marked by speaking in tongues. Instead, Spirit baptism is about the active pursuit of a life in the Spirit (Eph 5:18; Gal 5:25; Rom 8:14, 26). As such, Pentecostals testify to the fact that they are spiritually stronger, more receptive to the Spirit, and more active in Christian ministry than prior to the Spirit baptism.[10] The primary motivation for pursuing a dramatic life in the Spirit is nothing more than a passionate love of God. The early Pentecostals understood clearly that baptism in the Holy Spirit centered around a baptism in the love of God and a desire to be his missional ambassadors.[11]

Recognizing there was more of the Spirit available, Pentecostal experience historically came out of a deep dissatisfaction with things as they are in light of things as they were in the New Testament church. This

---

9. Vondey, *Pentecostal Theology*, 79.

10. Land, *Pentecostal Spirituality*, 168.

11. Yong, *Renewing Christian Theology*, 101.

dissatisfaction with spiritual apathy led to deep spiritual hunger to love God and pursue the moving of the Spirit in radical ways.[12] Concerning the Pentecostal perspective on Spirit baptism, Frank Macchia points out,

> Pentecostals rightly look at the prevalence of bench-warmers in the churches (including Pentecostal churches) and would encourage them to be baptized in the Spirit in dynamic praise and charismatic power for service toward others.

Therefore, for the Pentecostal, baptism in the Spirit functions as the immersion of human beings into divine love. This intimate experience causes the human spirit to be knit with the mission of the Spirit. In short, Spirit baptism is being filled with the love of God, motivating us toward that which God loves, lost humanity.

CONCLUSION

Scripture reveals that God intends for the works of the Holy Spirit to be discernible to humanity. Within the biblical narrative of Spirit baptism, speaking in tongues is seen as the repeated visible marker. Additionally, Spirit-inspired speech serves as token of the Spirit's transformative work within the Christian, empowering them for missional service. Simply put, speaking in tongues signifies an encounter with the divine and demonstrates that the Spirit possesses us, as opposed to the other way around, indicating an active participation with the Spirit.

For Pentecostals, Spirit baptism is viewed as a divine aid that equips them for missionary service and empowers them for a life of following the Spirit. Pentecostals seek Spirit baptism because they acknowledge their dependence on the Spirit for effective witnessing and because they desire to be prophetic voices in the world. While Spirit baptism does not make the Pentecostal better or more saved than the Christian who has never experienced Spirit baptism, they testify that it does enliven them with Spirit-inspired power and fuels their love for God and their commitment to his mission.

---

12. Fee, *Gospel and Spirit*, 108.

APPLICATION QUESTIONS

1. How might a posture of humility be involved in seeking Spirit baptism?

2. In what ways might Spirit baptism guard against spiritual apathy?

FURTHER READING

Dayton, Donald. *Theological Roots of Pentecostalism*. Grand Rapids: Baker Academic, 1987.

Hunter, Harold D. *Spirit Baptism: A Pentecostal Alternative*. Eugene, OR: Wipf & Stock, 2009.

Laurito, Timothy. *Speaking in Tongues: A Multidisciplinary Defense*. Eugene, OR: Wipf & Stock, 2021.

Macchia, Frank D. *Baptized in the Spirit: A Global Pentecostal Theology*. Grand Rapids: Zondervan Academic, 2009.

Menzies, William W., and Robert P. Menzies. *Spirit and Power: Foundations of Pentecostal Experience*. Grand Rapids: Zondervan, 2000.

McGee, Gary B., ed. *Initial Evidence: Historical and Biblical Perspectives on the Pentecostal Doctrine of Spirit Baptism*. Eugene, OR: Wipf & Stock, 2008.

Richie, Tony. *Essentials of Pentecostal Theology: An Eternal and Unchanging Lord Powerfully Present & Active by the Holy Spirit*. Eugene, OR: Wipf & Stock, 2020.

6

Perspectives on Missions

Pentecostals affirm that every disciple is called and empowered and every disciple is encouraged to expect that signs and wonders will accompany his or her witness.

—Paul Pomerville

INTRODUCTION

Lula Bell Hough (1906–2002) did not choose an easy or safe path in life. At age twenty-three, sensing God's call to ministry, she received credentials as an Assemblies of God missionary. Lula then left her comfortable life in America and devoted herself to sharing the gospel among the unreached people of southern China.

Hough's most significant challenge on the mission field came during World War II when she spent seven and a half months as a Japanese prisoner of war. During this time she lost over thirty-eight pounds, having nothing but wheat that was wormy and moldy to eat. Soldiers often placed their bayonets to her throat, threatening to kill her. She witnessed the death of thousands of her fellow prisoners, who were either murdered or starved to death.

Eventually, Hough was freed in a prisoner exchange—between American and Japanese prisoners of war. Upon her release, Lula continued her missionary work throughout southern China. For forty-five years, Hough ministered in areas with no gospel witness, enduring many hardships to ensure that these people heard about Jesus. She stated,

In some of these villages we were the first foreigners the villagers had ever seen, and in many, the first to preach the gospel. God has promised that His Word shall not return unto Him void, so we believe that if we are faithful in proclaiming the gospel, He will be faithful in drawing souls unto himself.[1]

What would motivate Hough (and many other early Pentecostal missionaries) to leave the comforts of the West and endure such unimaginable difficulties? What could possibly persuade a person to abandon "normal" sensibilities and embrace a lifestyle of immeasurable risk and self-denial? Why would anyone willingly choose to live in such a radical way? The answer is relatively simple. They felt a *personal responsibility* to be faithful to Christ in fulfilling the Great Commission.

"GO YE" MEANS ME

I will never forget lying awake in a hut near the Zambezi River deep in the bush of Zambia. The Zambezi is one of Africa's largest rivers, serving as the waterhole for countless elephants, hippopotami, lions, crocodiles, and all sorts of dangerous wildlife. As I lay awake imagining all the ways I might die, I thought, "What are you doing here? This is crazy! You should be at home, with your family, instead of out here in the middle of nowhere about to be a midnight snack for some animal." However, in the pitch-black African night, I suddenly remembered reading about the great missionary David Livingstone, who, while traveling throughout Africa, called the Zambezi River "God's Highway" because he believed that the Zambezi was the key to reaching the interior of Africa for Christ. At that moment, something powerful shifted in my spirit as I stopped focusing on the dangers around me and instead marveled at the immense privilege given to me to spread the gospel down "God's Highway."

One of Christ's final instructions to His followers was that they were to spread the gospel (good news) throughout the world to "make disciples of all the nations" (Matt 28:19). In establishing the church, Christ designed it to be an organization that is fundamentally focused on those who are not a part of it, commissioning the disciples to "Go into all the world and preach the gospel to all creation" (Mark 16:15). As the founder and leader of the church, Christ's missionary example serves as the guiding principle for all His followers for He "did not come to be served, but to serve, and to give

1. Hough, "Missionary Travels, S. China."

His life a ransom for many" (Matt 20:28). Christianity is a missionary movement because its founder was a missionary who came from heaven to save lost humanity.

> **Christianity is a missionary movement because its founder was a missionary who came from heaven to save lost humanity.**

It is evident from an examination of the Acts of the Apostles that the first disciples of Christ took their Master's command to spread the gospel as their *personal* mandate. The New Testament evidence is overwhelming that Christ's disciples believed they had an individual responsibility to go and spread the gospel of Christ throughout the known world. Commissioned by Christ and empowered by the Spirit, the disciples' obligation to spread the good news of Christ and His salvific work became their life's work. In a real sense, Christ's mission became their mission as they gave their lives proclaiming the gospel throughout the world and praying that "the Lord of the harvest to send out workers into His harvest" (Matt 9:38)

The word "mission" comes from the biblical Greek word for sending, highlighting the fundamental nature of Christianity as a sending religion. So foundational is Christ's mission mandate that countless followers of Christ throughout church history have willingly chosen to sacrifice and suffer immense persecution to evangelize the lost. Unashamedly providing a defense of the gospel, the Christian missionary combats false religions and argues for the superiority of Christ over other gods. These disciples of Christ voluntarily crossed cultural and linguistic boundaries, working tirelessly to communicate the gospel to those who had never heard its transformational truth.

Jesus commanded the first disciples to go to all the nations and gave them authority to "be My witnesses" (Acts 1:8). Along with authority, these early disciples were promised that the Spirit of God would empower them in their going. From the first disciples to our current time, every generation throughout the church age is called to the same responsibility of spreading the gospel message. With the same mission, authority, and power available in every generation, God continues to call today for those who will take ownership of this divine mandate and believe that the "Go ye" means me.

A PENTECOSTAL PERSPECTIVE

From the beginning of Pentecostalism, the movement has been marked by an urgency to spread the gospel to unreached people. The classical Pentecostal missionary effort was driven by a practical urgency of reaching the lost wherever they may be found. This recognition motivated early Pentecostals to make significant personal sacrifices toward reaching "even to the remotest part of the earth" (Acts 1:8).

The classical Pentecostal belief regarding Spirit baptism centered on its effectiveness for Spirit-enabled power to witness. Driven by the Spirit, Pentecostals have always been a missionary-focused group of people.[2] From their intense focus on the Spirit came an unquenchable passion for evangelizing the lost. At its core, the Spirit of Pentecost is the Spirit for others—the Spirit that motivates and empowers the church to bring the good news of Jesus to a lost and dying world.[3] Pentecostals see an integral connection between missions and the outpouring of the Holy Spirit on the day of Pentecost. Beginning with Peter's bold sermon, the Spirit's power enabled the disciples to launch Christ's command to "make disciples of all the nations" (Matt 28:19). For the Pentecostal, this Spirit-directed missional calling is the normative task of every believer.

> At its core, the Spirit of Pentecost is the Spirit for others—the Spirit that motivates and empowers the church to bring the good news of Jesus to a lost and dying world.

Pentecostal missiologist Allan Anderson offers six characteristics of Pentecostal missions:

> (1) Pneumatocentric mission, highlighting the role of the Holy Spirit in mission; (2) Dynamic mission praxis with zeal and commitment; (3) Evangelism as the central mission thrust; (4) Contextualization of leadership or development of local leadership as early as possible; and (5) Mobilization in mission where everyone

2. Yong, *Missiological Spirit*, 19.

3. Menzies, *Pentecost*, 36.

is called and empowered for witness; (6) Contextual missiology with creativity in packaging the gospel to be relevant to the local cultural and social setting.[4]

In simple terms, Anderson has observed that Pentecostal missiology: (1) emphasizes the central role of Spirit in missional efforts, (2) practices missions with great passion, (3) views the evangelism of the lost as the chief goal of missionary efforts; (4) prioritizes the quick development of local leaders, (5) believes in empowering all believers for missional witness, and (6) endeavors to make the gospel relevant within the culture. What is evident from this summarization is that a Pentecostal perspective of missions is more than an ancillary facet of Pentecostalism but is central to the DNA of the movement.

The Spirit DNA found within pentecostal missiology starts with the belief that a personal encounter with the missionary Spirit is available to all believers. Pentecostals have experienced enormous missional success worldwide, not just because they have utilized effective techniques, but because the primary distinctive of Pentecostal theology is the belief in a personal outpouring of the Holy Spirit into the life of each believer: a "personal Pentecost."[5]

So central is this idea within Pentecostalism that the motivating purpose for forming denominations was more than to articulate their distinctive doctrines but to facilitate missionary efforts. Born out of a sense of missional necessity, the Pentecostals organized to support foreign missions.[6] It was a Pentecostal reading of the Acts of the Apostles that caused them to believe that every disciple of Christ is capable (through Spirit empowerment) of obedience to Christ's missional command. Since Pentecostals use Acts as the paradigm through which they view their missional purpose, it is logical that they should expect to experience similar empowerment from the Spirit.[7]

As an Acts 29 community, Pentecostals view themselves as sharing the same message as the apostles: Jesus is Lord and Savior.[8] Pentecostal missiologist Paul Pomerville notes:

4. Anderson, "Towards a Pentecostal Missiology for the Majority World," 41.

5. McClung, "Truth on Fire", 82.

6. Menzies, *Spirit and Power*, 23.

7. Laurito, *Speaking in Tongues*, 58.

8. Menzies, *Pentecost*, 48.

> There is expectancy for the Spirit's ministry in mission today because the church is perceived to live and minister in the same salvation history time context as the New Testament church. On the basis of a biblical promise, Pentecostals look for a supernatural enablement and ministry in their own contemporary times, like the apostles and disciples experienced at the beginning of the missionary task.[9]

Pentecostals expect that the same Spirit that empowered the first-century church will empower the present-day church to be an effective missionary movement. The Pentecostal freely admits their utter dependence upon the Spirit's enablement to fulfill Christ's mission in today's world. Given the posture of complete reliance upon the Spirit's empowerment, it is no accident that modern Pentecostalism has grown exponentially since its humble beginnings at the start of the twentieth century.

For the Pentecostal, an integral part of a holistic vision of salvation involves being involved in the social concerns of humanity. Through investments in schools, hospitals, orphanages, disaster relief, feeding programs, and countless other humanitarian efforts, Pentecostals have not been oblivious to the practical needs of society. While accused by some outsiders as only being concerned with "heavenly" matters, Pentecostals have not been lazy in their efforts to better the condition of humanity and use compassion ministries as an evangelistic tool.[10]

Additionally, Pentecostals have traditionally sought the same missional power and experience that marked the early church. With unwavering confidence that they have been sent by the same missionary Spirit, Pentecostals depend on Spirit empowerment to fulfill the Great Commission and declare the "wonders of God" to the nations (Acts 2:11). This has led to a rapidly expanding missionary movement accompanied by miraculous signs and wonders. From a Pentecostal perspective, the day of Pentecost was not the day the church began but rather the day the church was empowered for missional effectiveness.

Embracing their Spirit-inspired mission, Pentecostals see themselves as end-time prophets who have been sent out as missionaries to the ends of the earth. Believing in the imminent (at any moment) return of Christ, the Pentecostal has a perspective on missions that is filled with urgency. Without question, the Pentecostal's view of missions is tied to their end-time theology. This age is the days of Spirit-empowered witness that conflicts with

9. Pomerville, *Third Force in Missions*, 75.

10. Kärkkäinen, "Mission in Pentecostal Theology," 15.

the forces of evil in a cosmic struggle that will culminate in the "last days."[11] Armed with Spirit empowerment and compelled by end-time urgency, the Pentecostal feels a Spirit-inspired awareness of their missionary calling.

The Pentecostal believes that if Spirit baptism at Pentecost resulted in the world's evangelization of that day, modern-day Spirit baptism is necessary for the evangelization of our world today. For Pentecostals, the missionary proclamation must go out to non-Christians and those who have once professed a Christian faith but now live a lifestyle indifferent to saving faith.[12] Believing that the Holy Spirit prepares people for the reception of the gospel, Pentecostals enthusiastically share the message of Jesus, knowing that the Spirit is working through their witness to reach those who have never heard the gospel since "faith comes from hearing, and hearing by the word of Christ" (Rom 10:17).

Accepting the same personal responsibility toward missions that marked the disciples of Christ, the Pentecostal embraces their Spirit-inspired calling to spread the gospel throughout the world—not out of compulsion, but motivated by a love for God. The Pentecostal witness is first and foremost driven by a passion for the kingdom of God and a love for the King. At its core, Pentecostal witness flows from Pentecostal worship.[13]

CONCLUSION

The missionary nature of Christianity stems from Christ's final command that His disciples share the gospel throughout the world and make disciples of all nations. The earliest disciples of Christ took this command seriously and believed it was their personal responsibility to spread the good news of Christ's redemptive work. In short, Christ's mission became their mission.

From its inception, Pentecostalism has been characterized by a sense of urgency to reach unreached people with the gospel. Driven by their reading of the Acts of the Apostles, Pentecostals viewed Spirit baptism as a necessity for Spirit-enabled witnessing power. At its essence, the Pentecostal sees the Holy Spirit's outpouring on the day of Pentecost as inseparably linked to the missional effectiveness experienced by the early church. Desiring the same working of the Spirit for their present day, the Pentecostal

11. Pomerville, *Third Force in Missions*, 889.

12. Cartledge, *Testimony in the Spirit*, 74.

13. Archer, *Gospel Revisited*, 42.

believes that Spirit baptism is essential for Spirit-led missional vocation and should be the normative lifestyle of every Christian.

Dependent upon the Holy Spirit, Pentecostals embrace their Spirit-inspired mission and view themselves as prophets of the end times who have been sent as missionaries to the ends of the earth. Accepting the same personal responsibility for missions as Christ's disciples, Pentecostals embrace their Spirit-inspired vocation to propagate the gospel around the world—not out of obligation, but out of a Spirit-inspired love for God. The Pentecostal witness is primarily motivated by a worshipful zeal for the kingdom of God and affection for God's mission in this world.

APPLICATION QUESTIONS

1. In what ways do you take Christ's mandate to spread the gospel personally?

2. How does a Pentecostal dependance on Spirit baptism for missional empowerment influence your thinking about the importance of Spirit baptism?

FURTHER READING

Anderson, Allan Heaton. *Spreading Fires: The Missionary Nature of Early Pentecostalism.* Maryknoll, NY: Orbis, 2007.

Dempster, Murray, Byron D. Klaus, and Douglas Petersen, eds. *The Globalization of Pentecostalism: A Religion Made to Travel.* Eugene, OR: Wipf & Stock, 2011.

Ireland, Jerry M. *The Missionary Spirit: Evangelism and Social Action in Pentecostal Missiology.* Maryknoll, NY: Orbis, 2021.

Lord, Andy. *Spirit-Shaped Mission: A Holistic Charismatic Missiology.* Carlisle, UK: Paternoster, 2005.

Ma, Julie C., and Wonsuk Ma. *Mission in the Spirit: Towards a Pentecostal/Charismatic Missiology.* Eugene, OR: Wipf & Stock, 2010.

Pomerville, Paul Anthony. *The Third Force in Missions: A Pentecostal Contribution to Contemporary Mission Theology.* Peabody, MA: Hendrickson, 2022.

Tyra, Gary. *The Holy Spirit in Mission: Prophetic Speech and Action in Christian Witness.* Downers Grove, IL: InterVarsity, 2011.

7

Perspectives on Worship

Pentecostalism is a diverse group of restoration-revivalistic movements held together by a common doctrinal commitment to the Full Gospel and experiential worship services.

—Kenneth J. Archer

INTRODUCTION

A friend of mine plays trumpet in a symphony orchestra. While I confess my knowledge of music is not the greatest, I greatly enjoy listening as he performs complex pieces of music. When I hear the beautiful melodies being played, I cannot help but think about how the components of an orchestra provide a wonderful analogy of worship. Every musician has a unique instrument and specific part to play, but they all work together toward a common goal—to create a beautiful and unified sound. Each musician dedicates a lifetime to honing their instrument so they can perform the music exactly as the composer intended. Additionally, an orchestra also needs a conductor to ensure that each musician works together as they play.

Similar to a composer, God has created the universe to proclaim a beautiful and unifying sound that praises His glory. Every atom of the universe shouts out the praises of God, "telling of the glory of God" (Ps 19:1). In a glorious act of grace, God has invited humanity to join in this cosmic symphony. While some have either rejected God or are ignorant of his invitation, many have accepted Christ's free gift of salvation and have joined the symphony of worshippers called the church. Like a skilled conductor, the Holy Spirit guides and motivates the church as it worships together so that this divine symphony exalts Christ and glorifies God the Father.

God created the human race specifically so that it could participate in divine fellowship since "God created man in His own image" (Gen 1:26). Having been invited to dwell within this divine fellowship, the creature is naturally motivated to worship the Creator. The fact that worship is an integral part of our human identity leads us to understand that worship was not conceived by humans but rather was an inspiration bestowed upon them by God. Therefore, it is essential to investigate the scriptural basis for worship in order to obtain a correct understanding of its significance and purpose.

BIBLICAL WORSHIP

Many modern Christians think about worship as primarily an event. They view worship as the performance done by a worship team during a Sunday morning church service or as a genre of Christian music. It has been noted that this narrow definition of worship has undermined worship within evangelicalism. There has been a tendency to trivialize worship through an excessive emphasis on atmospherics and mood, a misplaced focus on humanity rather than God, a lack of emphasis on the Word of God, the distortion of worship through emotional self-indulgence, and the exploitation of worship for market-driven purposes.[1] However, a biblical perspective on worship goes much deeper than an event or style of music. It reaches further than creating an atmosphere or emotion, but it actually has to do with a way of living that brings glory to God.

Biblical worship includes both acts of speech and physical performance that can occur in both public and private settings. Biblical worship is fundamentally the act of honoring, praising, and being devoted to God in response to His character, attributes, and works. The expression of worship takes many different forms, including prayer, singing, sacrifice, and obedience (Eph 5:19; Rom 12:1–2). Worship is intended to involve the complete person, as the follower of Christ is to love "the Lord your God with all your heart, and with all your soul, and with all your mind" (Matt 22:37). Many examples of worship can be found throughout the pages of Scripture, including David's psalms, the Old Testament's system of sacrifices, and the early church's sacred gatherings. All of these instances of worship are

1. Humphrey, *Grand Entrance*, 25.

marked by a fundamental posture of respect, awe, and appreciation for God's faithful kindness and merciful grace. As a result, the biblical concept of worship encompasses more than just the activity performed during a church service; it encompasses an entire way of life. It is too narrow a definition to think of worship only as something the Christian does; the biblical framework for worship gets to the heart of who we are—worshippers. Worship is more than just a means to a goal; rather, it is an end in and of itself. When we come to worship with the intention of receiving benefits, it ceases to be worship and instead transforms into an attempt to use God as a means to an end.

Worship language in the New Testament suggests a great deal about a Christian way of life and much less to do with the specific performances within the gathered assembly.

The Greek word for church denotes the gathered people of God. Although the word does not clearly state what this group will do, it does make it clear that they should live as those who have been chosen or called out by God. Because of this, the actions performed by this group are anything but ordinary. Worship language in the New Testament suggests a great deal about a Christian way of life and has much less to do with the specific performances within the gathered assembly.[2] Worship, then, in the New Testament is a comprehensive category describing the follower of Christ's total existence.[3] However, the lack of specific worship liturgy when it comes to New Testament gatherings has led some Christians to quarrel over the stylistic nature of true worship.[4]

2. McGowan, *Ancient Christian Worship*, 6.

3. Peterson, *Engaging with God*, 18.

4. Block, *For the Glory of God*, 27.

SPIRIT AND TRUTH

The account of Christ's conversation with the Samaritan woman at the well reveals the fact that worship of God should be shared equally by Jews and Gentiles. In revealing God's desire for authentic worshippers, Jesus said,

> But an hour is coming, and now is, when the true worshipers will worship the Father in spirit and truth; for such people the Father seeks to be His worshipers. God is spirit, and those who worship Him must worship in spirit and truth. (John 4:23–24)

Therefore, for humanity to worship God appropriately, we must begin by recognizing God's spiritual nature. Without a basic understanding of the spiritual dimension of God's essence, it becomes impossible to properly worship divinity. This highlights the reality that when we worship God, we are approaching a being who is fundamentally very different from ourselves. To say that God is spirit is to admit that He is immaterial, invisible, and infinite. This is in stark contrast to humans, who are material, visible, and finite.

Those who have been redeemed by Christ—having had their spiritual lives made alive—are those "who worship in the Spirit of God and glory in Christ Jesus and put no confidence in the flesh" (Phil 3:3). This does not eliminate the need for physical action in worship, but it does mean that the physical location or posture used in worship is not the thing that provides the spiritual nature of worship. Moreover, for worship to be performed "in truth," it requires that our spiritual worship conform to God's revelation in Scripture. Theology without worship is cold and lifeless; worship without theology is emotional and weak. Together, worship and theology can inspire a solid Christian faith and equip one to live a successful Christian life. Therefore, Christian doctrine ought to guide and inspire worship.[5] In short, to say that genuine worship can only be done in spirit and truth is to say that biblical worship is spirit/truth worship.

I will never forget an experience I had in Papua New Guinea that illustrated to me an important truth: not everything that presents itself as godly worship is in fact spirit/truth worship. I had been invited to preach at a large youth conference in which students from across the nation came together for a time of godly inspiration and spiritual renewal. During the worship time on the first night, I could not help but notice a young girl who was very demonstrative in her worship. Her passion and heartfelt expression of worship seemed to be so sincere and gave every impression of

---

5. Segler and Bradley, *Christian Worship*, 49.

coming from a genuine love for God. Yet, the moment I got up to preach the Word of God, she immediately started manifesting signs of demonic oppression. This sudden shift from passionate "worship" to demonic manifestation offered a helpful reminder that not all that appears godly on the surface is in fact spirit/truth worship. The authenticity of Christian worship is not measured by the fervor of our prayers or the intensity of our emotions, but by the reality of the Holy Spirit that lives within us.

A PENTECOSTAL PERSPECTIVE

Given the fact that the Pentecostal movement derives its identity from the outpouring of the Holy Spirit on the day of Pentecost, it should come as no surprise that Pentecostalism is famous for its emphasis on the experiential nature of worship. Viewing themselves as an Acts 29 community, Pentecostals look for the same workings of the Spirit found within the Acts of the Apostles.

Pentecostals are zealous in their pursuit of a worshipful encounter with the Holy Spirit because they are convinced that an experience with the Spirit is transformational.[6] Pentecostals do not view worship as simply a human activity. Worship includes a profound connection between the divine and humanity, a meeting. The practice of divine fellowship in worship is shaped by an attitude of anticipation. The Pentecostal anticipates that the Spirit will visit them. Therefore, the Pentecostal worship service has always been focused on an encounter with the Spirit. This has resulted in the attendee coming with a Spirit-inspired expectation that something supernatural will happen, and a belief that it will happen to them.[7]

> **Pentecostals are zealous in their pursuit of a worshipful encounter with the Holy Spirit because they are convinced that an experience with the Spirit is transformational.**

6. Boone, "Pentecostal Worship and Hermeneutics," 112.
7. Stephenson, "Pentecostalism and Experience," 197.

There are three main aspects of the Pentecostal perspective of worship: (1) worship as an expression of the Christian life, (2) worship as the entirety of the Pentecostal service, and (3) worship as a specific component within the gathering of believers. Moving from the broad to the narrow, the Pentecostal sees worship as the outflow of living a life in the Spirit that impacts every part of their life and Christian devotion. This perspective allows the Pentecostal to be quick to respond to the flow of the Spirit within a worship service. When the promptings or stirrings occur within the gathering of believers, the Pentecostal is open to moving in concert with the Spirit. This openness to move with the Spirit within a worship service is natural to the Pentecostal because they strive to live a life that moves in concert with the Spirit's leading as a way of life. While the Spirit initiates and guides worship, the Pentecostal seeks to be in step with the leading of the Spirit. In this way, the Pentecostal approaches worship with an attitude of expectancy: the Spirit will move God's people. It is this foundational understanding that shapes the style and structure of Pentecostal worship.

Therefore, the Pentecostal worshipper is not surprised when the Spirit moves in dramatic (even miraculous) ways both inside the church and outside of it. If the biblical framework for worship is centered around a way of life, then the heart of Pentecostal worship is a Spirit-empowered community that anticipates divine experiences in everyday life. To this point Pentecostal scholar Kenneth Archer writes,

> Early Pentecostal spirituality developed a distinct experiential theological tradition which was shaped christologically, grounded pneumatologically, and oriented eschatologically. Pentecostal theology is a theology of worship and witness because Pentecostal spirituality is a passion for the kingdom.[8]

Understanding their dependence on the Spirit to direct and inspire their lives of worship, the Pentecostal seeks to express their passion for the kingdom through the physical display of worship. Far more than mere ecstatic chaos, the Pentecostal views their worship as practicing for a time when they will worship in the fullness of the kingdom.

It is precisely this mindset of practicing their worship for an age to come that allows the Pentecostal to be open to worshipping God through a diverse range of practices. Summarizing the Pentecostal worship ethos, Kärkkäinen writes,

---

8. Archer, *Gospel Revisited*, 45.

> Pentecostal worshipping communities display their love of God through a wide variety of spiritual practices, such as tongues-speaking, prophetic utterances, healing prayers, and supernatural encounters with God.[9]

Even though Pentecostals are most known for embracing Spirit-inspired worship through speaking in tongues, it would be an error to limit Pentecostal worship to this one mode for the Pentecostal church exhibits Spirit-inspired worship in a number of different ways.

As worship led by the Holy Spirit, speaking in tongues (as a form of worship) provides a profound connection within worship. Speaking in tongues frees the human spirit from the constraints of language, enabling the worshipper to commune directly with the Holy Spirit. In addition, this type of worship increases receptivity to the Spirit's influence in worship and energizes the act of worship, resulting in the Pentecostal being more receptive to the Spirit's formation in other spheres of life.

Remember the illustration that began this chapter about classical music? Classical music depends on performing the song precisely as written by the composer. When the tempo and rhythms are performed in a style that fully replicates the notes on the page, the music is considered a success. However, Pentecostal worship is much closer to jazz music. Jazz is constructed within a flexible framework. This is not to suggest that it is chaotic (as described by some) because that would not be a fair characterization. Instead, jazz has a free-flowing flexibility that exists within an overarching consistent style of music. Just as a jazz composer assumes a spirit of freedom that empowers the music to change and develop in the moment, a Pentecostal worshipper has developed a sensitivity to the presence of the Spirit and a willingness to spontaneously change the "music" when the Spirit directs.[10]

Pentecostals (through speaking in tongues) not only benefit from this distinctive style of Spirit-inspired worship, but they also develop within them a distinctive way of thinking about worship. For the Pentecostal, speaking in tongues as a mode of worship (praising in tongues) is more than a novel way of worshipping; it is central to their identity and foundational to their purpose of worshiping God in spirit and in truth. The Pentecostal community engages in a beautiful type of free worship. However, within that freedom and spontaneity, there are clear guidelines

9. Kärkkäinen, *Introduction to Ecclesiology*, 13.

10. Félix-Jäger, *Spirit of the Arts*, 77.

that prevent worship from devolving into chaotic unloving sounds that resemble "a noisy gong or a clanging cymbal" (1 Cor 13:1). Pentecostal worship is characterized by the liberty to explore the glorious depths that exist in the relationship between the Word (structure) and the Spirit (freedom)[11]

CONCLUSION

The biblical view of worship transcends styles of music or locations of worship. Rather, for the Christian worship is a way of life that honors and praises God in response to His nature, attributes, and actions. Worship is meant to involve the whole person and is characterized by a fundamental posture of reverence, astonishment, and gratitude for God's goodness and grace.

In the New Testament, worship is a comprehensive category that describes the complete existence of a Christ-follower. Pentecostals emphasize a comprehensive experience of worship and desire a transformative encounter with the Holy Spirit through the act of worship. Due to their conviction that a worshipful encounter with the Holy Spirit is transformative, Pentecostals are zealous in their pursuit of this kind of experience. Pentecostals do not view worship as a purely human activity. In worship the Pentecostal finds a profound connection between humanity and the divine, a connecting of heaven and earth. The Pentecostal practice of speaking in tongues (as a form of worship) liberates the human spirit from the limitations of language, allowing the worshiper to communicate directly with the Holy Spirit.

APPLICATION QUESTIONS

1. Do you view worship as an activity done in church or as a way of life?

2. Do you possess a Spirit-inspired expectation that something supernatural will happen in worship? If not, why not?

---

11. Suurmond, *Word and Spirit at Play*, 88.

FURTHER READING

Archer, Kenneth J. *The Gospel Revisited: Towards a Pentecostal Theology of Worship and Witness*. Eugene, OR: Wipf & Stock, 2011.

Cartledge, Mark J., and A. J. Swoboda, eds. *Scripting Pentecost: A Study of Pentecostals, Worship and Liturgy*. London: Routledge, 2016.

Cox, Harvey Gallagher. *Fire from Heaven: The Rise of Pentecostal Spirituality and the Reshaping of Religion in the Twenty-First Century*. Cambridge, MA: Da Capo, 2007.

Félix-Jäger, Steven. *Renewal Worship: A Theology of Pentecostal Doxology*. Downers Grove, IL: InterVarsity, 2022.

Ingalls, Monique Marie, and Amos Yong, eds. *The Spirit of Praise: Music and Worship in Global Pentecostal-Charismatic Christianity*. University Park: Pennsylvania State University Press, 2015.

Martin, Lee Roy. *Toward a Pentecostal Theology of Worship*. Cleveland, TN: CPT, 2016.

8

Perspectives on Prayer

Spirit baptism means that from both bliss and sorrow, prayer becomes central to how we think and act in relation to God.

—FRANK MACCHIA

INTRODUCTION

Perhaps you have heard of the story about the bar in a small Texas town that began construction on a new building to increase their business. Securing land across from a little community church, the business owners went about building their tavern. Disgusted by the idea of a bar moving in across from their church, the congregation started praying for God to stop the bar from opening. However, work on the bar continued to progress right up until the day before its grand opening. That night a terrible storm blew across the town. During the course of the storm, lightning struck the bar, causing it to burn completely to the ground.

Upon hearing of the destruction of the bar, the congregation rejoiced because God had answered their prayers. However, their joy was short-lived for the bar owner promptly sued the church on the grounds that the church was ultimately responsible for the destruction of his building. In the lawsuit, the bar owner claimed that the church's actions of continual prayer caused the building to be destroyed. In its reply to the court, the church denied strongly that it was at fault or had anything to do with the building's destruction. When the time came for the judge to issue a verdict, he proclaimed,

> I do not know how I am going to rule in this case, because as it looks from the documents, we have a bar owner who believes in the power of prayer and an entire church congregation that does not.

Prayer, as a foundational act of faith, facilitates humanity's connection with divinity. If the purpose of humanity is to worship God, then the action of prayer provides a means for the creation to live within the design of the Creator. For the Christian, prayer is more than a cosmic wish but it is central to our identity as Christians. Prayer is not a last resort or desperate wish, but an act of power.

As divine communication, prayer's fundamental purpose is deeper than the exact words spoken in prayer. Due to our inherent human limitations in connecting with divinity, the language we choose in prayer has little influence on the success of our endeavor. Whether a person is using impressive theological words in their communication with God or offering up a simple prayer from their heart, the inherent power is not found in the proficiency of our vocabulary. Instead, the power originates with the Spirit of God connecting with our spirit and bring His divine life. Therefore, while the words themselves may have little ability, communicating with God is anything but powerless.

The primary reason why prayer is powerful is due to the person to whom we pray. We are not communicating with a stone idol or a mythical god, but rather with the eternal, triune God. As a result, prayer is effective solely on the basis that we are in communication with an omnipotent, omnipresent, all-knowing, and perfectly holy being. Prayer is effective because it establishes a connection between humanity and divinity, and as we are temples of the Holy Spirit, prayer facilitates an active uniting of heaven and earth. Given this divine connection, the action of prayer has the power to change humanity in profound ways.

WHEN YOU PRAY

Simply defined, prayer is a dialogical act between humanity and divinity. The concept of a personal relationship with God, however, is exclusive to the Christian worldview. For the Christian, to pray is to cultivate a relationship that enables a finite human being to connect with divine power.

Therefore, in a real sense, prayer is the first act that links faith and practice.[1] Prayer is a relationship of dialogue (not monologue) between God and a believer that has profound effects on every aspect of the pray-er. The purpose of this dialogue is not to change the immutable plans of God, but to help a believer to discern God's will and to taste of the mystery of divine relationship. Therefore, for mature Christians, prayer becomes less and less dependent on fleeces, feelings, or mysterious signs from God, and they trust more and more in the relationship built with a sovereign God.

Prayer is rooted in the idea of divine providence, which affirms a superior intelligence that controls the affairs of the universe. Prayer helps a believer to discover his or her place in God's design and to be in communion with God and the whole created universe, visible and invisible. Through the act of prayer, the pray-er begins to see God more fully and themselves as God's image-bearer. In divine communication, we humbly admit that we are not in control and that we are in desperate need of divine assistance for "it is He who has made us, and not we ourselves" (Ps 100:3). To neglect to pray is to contradict a fundamental truth of human existence: that the created requires the Creator. To fail to pray is to live in foolish self-dependence, arrogantly proclaiming, "There is no God" (Ps 53:1). In reality, a prayerless life is one of practical atheism. As people who live in and by the Spirit, prayer is that divine prompting of the Spirit that leads us to gratitude and petition in the Spirit. Whatever else life in the Spirit means, it must mean a life devoted to prayer.[2]

> **For mature Christians, prayer becomes less and less dependent on fleeces, feelings, or mysterious signs from God, and they trust more and more in the relationship built with a sovereign God.**

Prayer is made in a state of mind and heart that seeks God assistance in shaping the the pray-er's life to submit to God's will and power. Both the Old and New Testaments present prayer as a beautiful way of surrendering to God and offering worship. Within this framework, it is apparent that

1. Chan, *Spiritual Theology*, 125.

2. Fee, *People of God*, 53.

the purpose of prayer is to enable humanity to express gratitude for and worship of God. Prayer is the only appropriate response to realizing our incalculable debt to God for his lovingkindness and mercies. Because prayer involves communication with a divine being, the depth of prayer cannot be exhausted. Additionally, the scope of prayer is vast and includes adoration, thanksgiving, confession, and bringing our needs before God. As we adore God, offer our thanks, confess our sins, and bring our requests, we find ourselves being conformed into the image of Christ.

Christian prayer rejects fatalism but recognizes that through prayer, God's purposes can be revealed and accomplished. The goal of prayer is not to modify the will of God, but instead it is designed to aid the believer in submitting to the will of God. Therefore, one of the primary goals of prayer is to bring our will into alignment with the will of God. Similarly to how a chiropractor realigns the body, prayer realigns the spirit to surrender to God's will. The pattern of some Christians' prayers reveals that they believe God is nothing more than a cosmic genie. However, as the lifeblood of our relationship with God, prayer should not be done with a posture of selfishness but with the motivation of building a relationship with divinity. The prayers of a mature Christian progress further away from being self-centered petitions and closer to being prayers of adoration and gratitude.

Christians striving for maturity in their prayer life understand the importance of avoiding two extremes: not asking God for anything out of a fatalistic mindset, and thinking they can bend God's will to their own. The Christian must combine persistent prayer with an unwavering commitment to God's wise sovereignty.[3] While Christian prayer is not meant to twist God's arm into granting our requests, as a loving Father, God invites us to bring our needs before Him (Matt 7:7; 1 Peter 5:7; 1 John 5:14). Christian prayer is fundamentally characterized by petition because it accurately conveys the true nature of our dependence on God. It reminds the believer that God is the source of all goodness and that we, as finite beings, depend on God for everything.[4] It is for this reason that the Christian is persistent in prayer. It is not in order to make God do what we want, but through continuous prayer, God is able to train us toward cultivating a kingdom-of-heaven mentality. When God does not grant an answer to prayer quickly, often there is something God desires to do in us or with us before answering our prayer. When

---

3. Keller, *Prayer*, 137.

4. Carson, *Praying with Paul*, 13.

we view prayer through the lens of a dialogical relationship with God, we can more easily trust the answers God provides to our requests.

A PENTECOSTAL PERSPECTIVE

Pentecostal theology places an enormous premium on prayer as a major way of connecting with the presence of God.[5] Central to the Pentecostal practice of prayer is the belief that being filled with the Spirit is an essential aid. While all Christians pray in the Spirit, the Pentecostal distinctive practice of Spirit-inspired speech (through speaking in tongues) facilitates a radical openness and passionate zeal to communion in prayer. Pentecostalism has facilitated a revival within Christianity to the experiential nature of prayer.

Given that the Pentecostal movement gets its inspiration from the Acts of the Apostles, it is not surprising that Pentecostalism wants an experience equivalent to the outpouring of the Holy Spirit on the day of Pentecost in the present day. Pentecostals do not believe that the presence of the Holy Spirit is a static power. Instead, Pentecostals realize (at least implicitly) that as our spirit's sensitivity to the Spirit's movement increases, so does the intensity of the Spirit's manifestation. Driven by a commitment to seeking a contemporary experience in the Spirit, the Pentecostal prays with unwavering faith that the same Spirit that empowered the first church will empower our present generation to fulfill our Spirit-inspired mission.

Desperate for the manifestation of the Spirit in our world today, the Pentecostal will practice a type of persistent praying called "praying through." This type of praying places a focus on maintaining prayer until one receives a response from God. At its core, praying through originates from a heart that recognizes its desperate need for divine assistance. Similar to the disciples' commitment to remain in the upper room until they received Spirit baptism, the Pentecostal embraces an attitude of persistent prayer in desperation for divine action. This form of prayer is frequently accompanied by groanings that are inspired by the Holy Spirit, as well as lamentations and confessions (Rom 8:38).[6] At its core, the practice of persistent prayer for the Pentecostal is a type of prayer that comes from a yearning for the manifestations of the Spirit to assist them in their present struggles.

5. Richie, *Essentials of Pentecostal Theology*, 88.
6. Vondey, *Pentecostal Theology*, 86.

While Pentecostals certainly have a strong desire for all spiritual manifestations, they have discovered that the Spirit-inspired speech of speaking in tongues is more than just the sign of Spirit baptism; the practice also serves as a vital aid in prayer (1 Cor 14:2; Eph 6:18). The Pentecostal recognizes a significant transition in prayer from praying for the Spirit to praying in and with the Spirit. The Spirit-inspired action of speaking in tongues provides the Pentecostal with Spirit-induced confidence when praying in this mode. This confidence does not originate from themselves but rather from the Spirit, who empowers the "words" of their praying.

As with all forms of prayer, speaking in tongues has no spiritual power apart from the Holy Spirit. The only reason praying in tongues is spiritual is because of its connection with the Holy Spirit. Yet, speaking in tongues (when initiated by the Spirit) is a powerful form of prayer because it is prayer guided by the Spirit. Since speaking in tongues transcends human understanding, it is prayer that originates with the Spirit and flows through our spirit. This does not mean that the Spirit takes over a person's will and forces them to pray in tongues; instead, the scriptural pattern indicates that the Spirit prays in union with our human will to pray. In addressing the fact that speaking in tongues works in unity with our human will, the apostle Paul talks about his personal prayer life stating, "I will pray with the spirit and I will pray with the mind also (1 Cor 14:15).

The Pentecostal understands that speaking in tongues as a mode of prayer has no magical abilities. Instead, its power comes from connecting our spirit to the Holy Spirit through this mode of prayer. The Pentecostals' willingness to speak in tongues demonstrates their innate understanding that the words used in prayer have no effect on the power of the action of prayer. Instead, the spiritual power gained through prayer comes only through the Spirit.[7]

> **As with all forms of prayer, speaking in tongues has no spiritual power apart from the Holy Spirit. The only reason praying in tongues is spiritual is because of its connection with the Holy Spirit.**

7. Laurito, *Speaking in Tongues*, 53.

Because praying in tongues is a mode of prayer that transcends human limitations, Pentecostals value the way this kind of prayer transforms their praying. This mode of prayer, which begins with the Spirit and flows through the pray-er's spirit, cannot help but transform the pray-er in significant ways. Having experienced God's presence through Spirit-inspired prayer, the Pentecostal testifies to the incredible benefits that come from this mode of prayer. Most notably, the Pentecostal finds praying in tongues to be an effective weapon in spiritual battles (Eph 6:18; Jude 1:20). The Pentecostal recognizes that praying in the Spirit is a spiritual weapon that assists them in their weaknesses (Rom 8:26–27), opens their discernment to comprehend the mindset of the Spirit (1 Cor 2:10–16), and helps shape their will to God's purposes (Eph 1:17–18).

CONCLUSION

Prayer is a dialogue between God and the Christian that has profound effects on every aspect of the pray-er's life. It facilitates the Christian's discovery of their place in God's design and fellowship with the Designer. Prayer enables humanity to convey gratitude and worship for God. Through prayer, Christians align their will with God's will, not to alter it but to submit to it.

Fundamental to a Pentecostal perspective on prayer is the conviction that being baptized with the Holy Spirit is an indispensable aid in prayer. While all Christians pray in the Spirit, the distinctive Pentecostal practice of Spirit-inspired speech (through speaking in tongues) facilitates a radical openness and intense devotion to prayer.

The Pentecostal prays with confidence that the exact same Spirit who empowered the first church will empower our current generation to accomplish our Spirit-inspired mission. At its foundation, the Pentecostal practice of persistent prayer is a form of prayer that yearns for the manifestations of the Holy Spirit to aid in their present struggles. Most notably, Pentecostals believe that praying in tongues is an effective spiritual weapon in spiritual warfare and an empowering force in their spiritual life.

APPLICATION QUESTIONS

1. Do you view prayer as a means of getting what you want from God or as an opportunity to build a relationship with God?

2. Can you testify to the transformational nature of Spirit-inspired praying? If so, how has it transformed your prayer life?

FURTHER READING

Archer, Kenneth J. *The Gospel Revisited: Towards a Pentecostal Theology of Worship and Witness*. Eugene, OR: Wipf & Stock, 2011.
Batterson, Mark. *The Wild Goose Chase: Reclaiming the Adventure of Pursuing God*. Colorado Springs, CO: Multnomah Books, 2008.
Wilkinson, Michael, and Peter Althouse. *Catch the Fire: Soaking Prayer and Charismatic Renewal*. DeKalb, IL: Northern Illinois University Press, 2014.

9

Perspectives on Spiritual Disciplines

Ritual practices, revivals, personal piety, and ascetic discipline, although often with stronger emphasis on the individual, are the tributaries to sanctification from a Pentecostal viewpoint.

—Wolfgang Vondey

INTRODUCTION

In the early 2000s, a young Kenyan runner named Eliud Kipchoge dreamed of becoming a marathon runner. Despite growing up in poverty and facing numerous obstacles, including a lack of access to proper training facilities and equipment, Kipchoge remained determined to succeed.

He began his training at a local high-altitude training facility, where he concentrated on improving his endurance and speed through demanding workouts and long-distance runs. Despite the challenges of training at high altitude, Kipchoge continued to push himself, frequently running more than one hundred miles per week. His devotion and hard work paid off when he won his first major marathon, the Berlin Marathon, in 2003. Kipchoge went on to win numerous marathons and set course records in Chicago, London, and Berlin in the years that followed. Kipchoge's biggest accomplishment, however, came in 2019, when he became the first person in history to run a marathon in under two hours, finishing in one hour, fifty-nine minutes, and forty seconds. The accomplishment was the culmination of years of hard work and preparing his body to endure the demands of long-distance running.

Kipchoge's incredible achievement has inspired runners all across the world to prepare and practice so that they can be the greatest athletes they can be. His story illustrates the effectiveness of a disciplined lifestyle, which enabled him to overcome significant difficulties in order to achieve a specific goal: winning a race.

Just as the athlete must train to be successful in their objective, so the Christian must be a person who learns to train (disciplines) themselves "for the purpose of godliness" (1 Tim 4:7). Soul training is the life's work of the disciple of Christ. The biblical (as well as practical) cure for unrighteous living is to fill our life with the life of the Spirit (Eph 5:18; Gal 5:16; 2 Cor 3:18). Throughout Paul's letters, he often compares the Christian life to that of an athlete who is striving for a prize (1 Cor 9:24–27; Phil 3:13–14; Gal 2:2; 5:7; 2 Tim 4:7). Paul's primary objective in adopting athletic metaphors is to teach Christian disciples the necessity of spiritual discipline in achieving their ultimate purpose. By staying focused on the goal, the athlete is able to discipline themselves in the midst of pain and difficulty, knowing that the present suffering will be worthwhile in the end. Embedded in this metaphor is the important biblical truth that entry in the Christian life does not ensure winning; remaining faithful to Christ requires both discipline and perseverance (Matt 24:13; Heb 10:38).[1]

SPIRITUAL/PHYSICAL BEINGS

As human beings, we are designed by God to consist of a duality of a spiritual and a physical nature. The spiritual and physical components of our being are so intricately intertwined that only death can separate them. Given the spiritual and physical nature of our existence, it is undeniable that the convergence of these two realities brings about a duality of cause and effect. In other words, the spiritual aspect of our identity will influence our physical life, and our physical actions will impact our spiritual dimension. A biblical understanding of human nature should prepare us to recognize that within every spiritual act there is a physical component, and conversely, within every physical activity there is a spiritual component (1 Cor 6:20; Rom 12:1).

---

1. Fee, *First Epistle to the Corinthians*, 480.

Prior to conversion, the spiritual component of our existence was "dead in your trespasses and sins" (Eph 2:1). However, upon salvation, the Spirit of God makes alive the spiritual nature within us and makes us born again (John 3:3; 2 Cor 5:17; 1 Pet 1:23). This new life enables the spiritual part of our nature to influence our physical existence in radically different ways. Therefore, in a very real sense, for salvation to impact our lives, it must involve physical change. To exclude our physical body from the work of salvation is to prevent salvation from working in our life. The surrendering of our life to Christ is inseparable from the giving up of our physical body so that it can be used for God's glory (John 14:23; 1 Cor 6:5–20; Eph 2:22).[2] Many modern Christians have (whether intentionally or unintentionally) created a dichotomy of their life, separating their spiritual life from their physical life as though each can function independently of the other. This devastating error has resulted in innumerable Christians possessing a head full of information about Christ but a physical body that is incapable of obeying Christ's commands. The marker of Christian maturity is about more than knowing correct theology but involves the continual training of our body to practice godly living.

> **Therefore, in a very real sense, for salvation to impact our lives, it must involve physical change. To exclude our physical body from the work of salvation is to prevent salvation from working in our life.**

Central to the topic of spiritual disciplines is the human will. C. S. Lewis, the famous Christian apologist and novelist, once observed,

> Every time you make a choice you are turning the central part of you, the part of you that chooses, into something a little different from what it was before And taking your life as a whole, with all your innumerable choices, all your life long you are slowly turning this central thing either into a heavenly creature or into a hellish creature: either into a creature that is in harmony with God, or else into one that is in a state of war and hatred with God. To be the one kind of creature is heaven: that is joy and peace and knowledge

2. Willard, *Spirit of the Disciplines*, 31.

and power. To be the other means madness, horror, idiocy, rage, impotence, and eternal loneliness. Each of us at each moment is progressing to the one state or the other.[3]

While the shift from spiritual death to spiritual life occurs instantly at the time of conversion, the effort of altering the habits of the will from ungodly passions to godly desires involves the continuous activity of the Holy Spirit in collaboration with our own will. This ongoing conformity of our decisions to godliness cannot occur without physical effort. In other words, the Christian does not observe this process passively. If a Christian is to train themselves for a life of righteousness, he or she must adopt bodily habits that will influence their spiritual life. As discussed in chapter 4, a person who wants to follow Christ must "count the cost" (Luke 14:26–33). Therefore, every Christian must be willing to embrace the physical formation involved in their spiritual journey. As C. S. Lewis pointed out, this choice is not a one-time decision. Instead, it is a continual choice to surrender control of our body to that which will build our spiritual life (Luke 9:23; Gal 5:27; 1 Cor 9:27).

Remember the athlete illustration from the beginning of the chapter? Imagine an enthusiastic young boy who aspires to play football. He has watched football games, and the sport looks just like something he would like to be involved in. So, the young boy begins to dream of making it to the National Football League. He pictures himself as a professional athlete capable of winning numerous awards and championships. However, a startling reality interrupts this glorious daydream. In order to accomplish this dream, there is going to be tremendous sacrifice involved. He must put in countless hours of training at the gym, lifting incredibly heavy weights. This goal will require him to endure endless summer days of training his body while sweating in oppressive heat. He will have to spend years studying the game, learning techniques and strategies to improve his abilities. There is a great risk of significant injury, which could require surgeries and months of physical therapy. It is in this moment that the young boy understands an important principle: any prize cannot be divorced from the cost of physical pursuit.

The athlete disciplines their body so that it can effectively respond to the demands of their sport. Similarly, Christians must condition their bodies to respond in a manner consistent with God's kingdom. At this point, it is crucial that we recognize that the spiritual training of our bodies for

3. Lewis, *Mere Christianity*, 86.

godly living does not increase God's love for us. From beginning to end, the Christian life is wholly dependent on God's grace. It is only because of the grace of God that the Spirit desires to shape our desires toward godliness.[4] Some view spiritual disciplines as an instrument for gaining God's favor or attaining righteousness. They engage in spiritual disciplines in order to improve their standing with God. This mindset reveals an error in their understanding of both salvation and the purpose of spiritual disciplines.

The ultimate purpose for practicing spiritual disciplines is to train our bodies to respond in Christ-honoring ways. As participators in God's divine kingdom, Christ invites us to take on the yoke of living like Him: "Take My yoke upon you and learn from Me, for I am gentle and humble in heart, and you will find rest for your soul. For My yoke is easy and My burden is light" (Matt 11:29–30). The action of spiritual disciplines is a type of rehearsing that helps us form a way of life that is practicing (for) the kingdom.[5] The formation of such a lifestyle necessitates the constant submission of our bodies to a different pattern of living than what we were accustomed to before following Christ. Therefore, the ultimate goal for practicing spiritual disciples must be twofold: the destruction of the "body of sin" (Rom 6:6) and the cultivation of the life of the Spirit that produces fruit and gifts in the believer (Gal 5:22–25; 1 Cor 12:4–11). Any motivation outside of these presents a real danger that spiritual disciplines produce self-righteousness pride and thereby lose their spiritual utility.

While spiritual disciples do nothing to help us earn our relationship with God, at the same time, it is equally crucial to understand that spiritual disciplines aid us in our capacity to love and obey God's commands. By stripping away physical appetites, our spiritual appetites are able to become stronger. When we sacrifice natural desires, we discover that our spiritual desires grow as our affections go beyond physical bread for: "Man shall not live on bread alone, but on every word that proceeds out of the mouth of God" (Matt 4:4). In this way, spiritual disciplines serve as a guard against the Christian experiencing love drift. Scripture repeatedly warns of the perils of our affections straying from Christ (Col 3:2–3; 1 John 2:15–17; Rev 2:4). Adopting a spiritually disciplined Christian lifestyle enables us to continue to prioritize our devotion to Christ. In the end, spiritual disciplines are a tool that keeps our appetites focused on Christ, and as a result, our whole being is shaped into God's character and likeness.

---

4. Mathis, *Habits of Grace*, 37.

5. Smith, *Desiring the Kingdom*, 212.

SHAPING SAINTS

Having discussed the purpose and necessity of spiritual disciplines, it is essential to provide a brief summary of these grace-filled habits. There is no standardized list of spiritual disciplines; however, some have developed a threefold typology of inward disciplines (meditation, prayer, fasting, and study), outward disciplines (simplicity, solitary, submission, and service), and corporate disciplines (confession, worship, guidance, and celebration).[6] Others have classified spiritual disciplines into two groups: disciplines of abstinence (solitude, silence, fasting, frugality, chastity, secrecy, and sacrifice) and disciplines of engagement (study, worship, celebration, service, prayer, fellowship, confession, and submission).[7] In addition to providing a framework for contemplating spiritual disciplines, categorizing spiritual disciplines reveal the variety and complexity of the exercise.

Such a list may appear overwhelming and unattainable to a new Christian or to a follower of Christ who has never practiced spiritual disciplines. The purpose of identifying the diversity of spiritual disciplines is to emphasize the options and depths available to the practitioner, rather than to induce feelings of intimidation or inadequacy. Remember these are habits of grace, not habits of perfection. Far too often, Christians approach spiritual disciplines as if it was an all-or-nothing practice. They mistakenly believe that unless they immediately achieve their goal in practicing a spiritual discipline, then it has failed. But success or failure should not be judged in such a rigid, black-and-white manner.

For example, say that a follower of Christ is prompted by the Spirit to begin practicing the spiritual discipline of fasting. Being new to the practice, they desire to set an ambitious goal of fasting three days. However, on the second day they no longer have the will to continue, and they break their fast. Was the practice of fasting a failure? Did the fact that they fasted less than they intended mean the practice lost its spiritual value? I certainly think not! While there is nothing inherently wrong with setting markers that help establish boundaries for disciplines, the successfulness of spiritual disciplines must go deeper than such markers.

All this to say, whether you have experience with practicing spiritual disciplines or would judge yourself a novice, there is opportunity for every Christian to experience spiritual growth through these practices of grace.

6. See Foster, *Celebration of Discipline.*
7. See Willard, *Spirit of the Disciplines.*

The nature of our human existence coupled with the scope and depth of spiritual disciplines make it possible for continual growth and "pressing on toward the goal" of Christlike living (Phil 3:12–16). After all, the purpose of practicing spiritual disciplines is not to compare the growth of one another but to facilitate the continual shaping of our lives into the image of Christ: "But we all, with unveiled face, beholding as in a mirror the glory of the Lord, are being transformed into the same image from glory to glory, just as from the Lord, the Spirit" (2 Cor 3:18). When it comes to being shaped into the image of Christ, every saint needs continued shaping.

A PENTECOSTAL PERSPECTIVE

Historical Pentecostals, although poor in material wealth, were characterized by being rich in spiritual matters. As a result of the life-altering power of the Holy Spirit, Pentecostals rapidly developed into a community of believers who emphasized spiritual disciplines. The early Pentecostals were interested in building a spiritually powerful community, and their reading of Scripture led them to find a clear correlation between this goal and spiritual disciplines.[8]

From the beginning of Pentecostalism, the significance of "emptying out," "putting off," or "killing" the flesh was acknowledged as critical. This type of dying language was adopted to describe the role of spiritual disciplines in denying carnal appetites. Such actions were not undertaken in order to become deserving of God's favor or to attain some super-elite level of spirituality. Instead, they were intended to help the Pentecostal give God more of their affection and attention. They were embraced in order to willfully eliminate things that could lead the Christian away from God's nature and will.[9] For the Pentecostal, encountering the Spirit as an active force in their life keeps them hungry for more of the Spirit and motivates their willingness to embrace spiritual disciplines.

Just as with other Christians, the Pentecostal does not pursue spiritual disciplines simply for the sake of knowing about God or theological understanding of mystical practices. Instead, driven by the desire for a dynamic experience with God, the Pentecostal is well suited to being open to the Spirit's work through spiritual disciplines. Possessing a profound passion for the Spirit, the Pentecostal is inherently open to the radical pursuit of

8. Menzies, *Pentecost*, 135.

9. Land, *Pentecostal Spirituality*, 168.

spiritual experiences. When this desire is channeled through spiritual disciplines, Pentecostal spirituality offers a beautiful structured freedom.

This notion of structure freedom is not an illogical idea. Have you ever watched a skilled athlete perform their craft? Perhaps you have seen a world-class athlete competing and wondered how they do it. The answer lies in the structure of freedom that exists in sports. On the surface, it may seem like athletes are completely free to do whatever they want on the field or court. However, this is not entirely true. Athletes operate within a carefully designed framework that allows them to perform at their highest level. This structure of freedom is built upon years of training and practice. Athletes learn the fundamental techniques and strategies of their sport, mastering the basic skills that allow them to compete at a high level. Once they have a solid foundation, they are then free to push the boundaries of what is possible within the constraints of the game. The structure of freedom in sports allows athletes to express themselves fully within the rules of the game. It is a delicate balance that requires both discipline and creativity. And when it all comes together, it is truly a thing of beauty to witness.

> **Possessing a profound passion for the Spirit, the Pentecostal is inherently open to the radical pursuit of spiritual experiences.**

Likewise, the Pentecostal who adopts a lifestyle of spiritual disciplines can enjoy the freedom to explore infinite depths of the Spirit while ensuring they remain safe within the home of orthodox Christian practices of discipleship. Guided by a belief that the Spirit will fill all who "hunger and thirst for righteousness" (Matt 5:6), the Pentecostal can eagerly explore the limitlessness of the Spirit's empowerment while remaining tethered to Christian practices that have proven effective for spiritual growth throughout church history. Cultivating habits of grace enables the continued development of a lifestyle that senses the Spirit's presence working both within them and around them while guarding the Pentecostal against looking to extra-biblical practices as a means of attaining spiritual growth.

Within the Pentecostal ethos there is an expectation for a daily vital experience of placing oneself at the disposal of the Spirit as the author of and guide of life. The disciplines of private and corporate prayer, reading the Holy Scriptures, living in fellowship with other believers, the Lord's Supper, and fasting are all ways of learning to attend to the Spirit in following Christ. For Pentecostals, being filled with the Spirit is a way of talking about the integration of these aspects into the Christian life,[10] an integration designed to unite God's will and ours in a mutual loving relationship. In this way, the practice of spiritual disciplines heightens the Pentecostal's awareness to the Spirit's activity in all things and guides their efforts to grow in a loving relationship with God.

CONCLUSION

Spiritual disciplines are intended to train our bodies to respond in Christ-honoring ways and to cultivate a Spirit-led existence that produces spiritual fruit and gifts in the believer. The effort of altering the habits of the will from ungodly passions to godly desires involves the continuous activity of the Holy Spirit in collaboration with our own will. These grace-filled practices enhance our ability to love and heed God's commands. Spiritual disciplines are habits of grace, not of perfection; therefore, success and failure should be evaluated in grace. Within a framework of grace, spiritual disciplines are intended to facilitate the ongoing transformation of our lives into the image of Christ, and every Christian requires ongoing spiritual transformation.

Spiritual disciplines are emphasized in Pentecostalism as a means to deny carnal desires and draw closer to God. Spiritual disciplines allow Pentecostals to explore the limitless dimensions of the Spirit while remaining tethered to canonical Christian practices. The incorporation of spiritual disciplines into the Pentecostal's life heightens their awareness of the Spirit's activity and is intended to lead them toward an intimate relationship with the Spirit.

10. Land, *Pentecostal Spirituality*, 176.

APPLICATION QUESTIONS

1. What might change in your spiritual journey by beginning to practice spiritual disciplines?

2. Who might you ask to join you in pursuing a lifestyle of spiritual disciplines?

FURTHER READING

Cartledge, Mark J. *The Mediation of the Spirit: Interventions in Practical Theology.* Pentecostal Manifestos. Grand Rapids: Eerdmans, 2015.

Chan, Simon. *Pentecostal Theology and the Christian Spiritual Tradition.* London: A&C Black, 2000.

Land, Steven Jack. *Pentecostal Spirituality: A Passion for the Kingdom.* London: A&C Black, 1993.

McNicol, Bruce, et al. *The Kingdom Life: A Practical Theology of Discipleship and Spiritual Formation.* Carol Stream, IL: Tyndale House, 2016.

10

Perspectives on Spiritual Gifts

The gifts of the Spirit are not optional extras for the Christian life, but essential tools for effective ministry.

—Donald Gee

INTRODUCTION

I once read of a kind man who realized that one of his friends was experiencing financial difficulty. The benevolent man went to his friend and offered him an old painting, telling him that if he made use of it, it would solve all of his money issues.

A few months later, the man observed that his friend still seemed to be in need of money. It was apparent that his friend still seemed very stressed, and there were no indications that his financial status had changed. Interested in what was going on, he went to his friend's house.

"What happened? Was the gift I provided you not enough to cover your expenses?" the generous man asked, puzzled at the situation.

Going over to the closet, his friend pulled out the old painting and responded, "Well, I appreciate you trying to help me, but when I started looking at the painting, I realized it was very old and it looked like it probably was not worth very much. I did not want to embarrass you if I tried to sell this old thing and it turned out to be not very valuable."

In disbelief, the generous man shook his head and said, "Friend, this painting is a masterpiece that is worth hundreds of thousands of dollars. While it may look old and useless, it is in fact an incredibly rare piece of art. Not only this, but it was painted by my great-great-grandfather and has been passed down through my family for centuries."

Disappointed and offended at the arrogance of his friend's unwillingness to use the gift that he had so kindly provided, the generous man took his priceless picture and left the needy man to struggle on his own.

Just like the man in the story illustrates, some Christians hold a cessationist perspective on spiritual gifts and reject the value of spiritual gifts. Cessationism states that the gifts of the Spirit were limited to the apostolic period and have since ceased operating within the church. Such a perspective on spiritual gifts suggests that what the Spirit gave to the first church, the Spirit withholds from the modern church.

Those that hold to such a belief look at spiritual gifts as antiques of biblical times necessary for the church in that age because they did not have the New Testament writings. However, such a perspective ignores the teachings of the New Testament about spiritual gifts and underestimates the currents church's need for spiritual gifts. The New Testament offers no indication that the spiritual gifts that were in operation in the first church were intended by God to only be for the Christians of the first church. Additionally, it is arrogant to assume that the present church does not need the spiritual gifts that God provided for them.

In contrast, Pentecostals are known for resisting any and all attempts to limit spiritual gifts to the first century or to deny the reality of the miraculous workings of the Spirit. The Pentecostal perspective views the biblical and historical evidence as quite clear: spiritual gifts are for all periods of the church. Although the charismatic gifts remained prevalent throughout much of the first two centuries of the Christian era, extant records indicate their diminishment during the third century. The gifts seem to have become less important in the life and thinking of the church as it became more organized.[1] However, this "ceasing" of spiritual gifts was not because God intended for them to stop or because there is a scriptural case to be made for their ceasing. Instead, spiritual gifts diminished because of a failure within the church and a controlling of manifestations by religious leaders.

---

1. Yong, *Renewing Christian Theology*, 62.

GIVEN FOR THE CHURCH

Spiritual manifestations are a revealing of that which the Spirit desires to accomplish in the physical. The Spirit is constantly working within the community of believers, but all that the Spirit does is not always seen through visible means. Spiritual manifestations are necessary to make the invisible visible to the church. As the Spirit works through the various gifts of grace, the church is able to tangibly experience the undeniable presence of God. These gifts of grace are not given as some reward because Christians earn God's favor, but are given by the Spirit to "each one individually just as He wills" (1 Cor 12:11).

The process of making visible that which the Spirit desires within the local assembly is not intended to be chaotic or random confusing acts, "for God is not a God of confusion (1 Cor 14:33). Therefore, it is necessary that spiritual manifestations operate within a biblical framework. In addressing how spiritual manifestations should operate within the church, the apostle Paul outlines three frameworks in 1 Corinthians 12–14: (1) diversity within unity, (2) order for edification, and (3) the priority of love.

These frameworks allow for the whole range of spiritual manifestations to function in a loving manner designed to help build up the church and ensure they operate "properly and in an orderly manner" (1 Cor 14:40). To miss any one of these frameworks results in spiritual manifestations missing the mark. At the center of spiritual manifestation, guiding and motivating their proper function, is the priority of love. To this point Amos Yong writes,

> Not only are the manifestations nothing without love (13:2–3), but love neither ends nor fails (13:8), and it remains the greatest (13:13) expression of the church. Fundamentally the desire for the manifestation of the Spirit should be encouraged only if the members of the body follow and pursue after the way of redemptive love (14:1).[2]

In short, spiritual gifts, no matter how spectacular and exciting, have no spiritual value and can even become destructive if they are not administered in love. However, when motivated by love, spiritual gifts empower the church to perform spiritual acts of unified worship and service.

The underlying purpose of the spiritual gifts is to help build up the church. Therefore, if the action of some manifestation is done without the

---

2. Yong, *Renewing Christian Theology*, 71.

motivation of edifying or profiting the church, then the action no longer retains its spiritual value: "So also you, since you are zealous of spiritual gifts, seek to abound for the edification of the church" (1 Cor 14:12). For Paul, the gathered community of worship should seek to cultivate a culture that respects and loves that which is good for the whole, not to primarily seek individualistic spirituality. In the case of the Corinthians their pursuit of individualistic spirituality had led to a false spirituality altogether.[3] Rather than spiritual gifts being about the benefit of the whole church, the self-promoting and self-centered approach of the Corinthians had led to the inversion of these gifts from spiritual to unspiritual. For manifestations that are motivated by self-promotion, arrogance, and other ungodly motives lose their spiritual value no matter how spiritual they may appear.

Spiritual gifts, no matter how spectacular and exciting, have no spiritual value and can even become destructive if they are not administered in love.

It is evident that spiritual gifts are not about the personal edification of the giver, but about the building up of the whole church. Spiritual manifestations that are done to promote an ungodly agenda or with some self-centered motivation are like the person who wants to give a gift with strings attached. When this happens, the gift is no longer given purely for the enjoyment and benefit of someone else. Instead, the gift becomes tainted with motivations and agenda's that prevent the value of the gift from being fully enjoyed and beneficial to the recipient. The purity of spiritual manifestations is ensured when they are given with the intent of building up the entire community of believers.

Paul centers his entire teaching about spiritual gifts around the understanding that they are to be used "for the common good" (1 Cor 12:7). This framework ensures that spiritual manifestations occur as an outflow of love. Desiring to see the community of believers obtain all that the Spirit desires, the person operating in a spiritual gift does so in order that others will be built up and not themselves. In a very fundamental sense, the operation of

---

3. Fee, *First Epistle to the Corinthians*, 636.

gifts is not about the person who is being used by the Spirit, but about aiding the whole church to better fulfill its divine mission. Through spiritual gifts, that which the Spirit-empowered church needs is provided.[4] As such, the gifts of the Spirit are given to aid the church in fulfilling its mission: to glorify Christ and evangelize the lost. The gifts do not exist for the church to congratulate itself on its ability to operate in supernatural manifestations. Rather, the gifts of the Spirit are meant to build up the church and to better equip it to stay on its Spirit-inspired mission.

While the gifts of the Spirit are designed to build or edify the church, this does not mean the effect of their operation should be regulated to a church building or service. In other words, the impact of spiritual manifestations that take place within the fellowship should reach outside the fellowship of believers. Since their beginnings, Pentecostals have promoted a Spirit-centered theology of mission and evangelism, contending that spiritual manifestations are designed to direct believers toward Spirit-inspired mission.[5]

Given the innumerable ways in which the Spirit is capable of working within this world, it makes sense that it would require a diversity of spiritual manifestations to express the actions of God through the church. In setting up his discussion on spiritual gifts, Paul emphasizes that there are different kinds of gifts, but they all come from the same Spirit, Lord, and God. The diversity within unity found within spiritual gifts is connected to the diversity within unity that is found within the triune Godhead. Just as there are three distinct persons but one God, so there are various distinct gifts but they all have the same divine source.

Through spiritual manifestations, the fellowship of believers experiences a divine awareness of the prophethood of all believers, resulting in the Spirit-inspired activity of the church moving beyond the religious elite and being experienced by every believer (Acts 2:17–18; 1 Cor 12:13; 1 Pet 2:9).[6] In a day where spiritual gifts operating within the church laity seem to be declining, the current trend favoring spiritual manifestations only coming from pastoral leadership, a Pentecostal perspective that rejects the centralizing of spiritual manifestations is needed. This decentralizing of the Spirit's activity is realized through the diversity of spiritual gifts working together to accomplish the Spirit's purposes. In other words, it is the belief

4. Macchia, *Tongues of Fire*, 237.

5. Yong, *Discerning the Spirit(s)*, 220.

6. Stronstad, *Prophethood of All Believers*, 113.

in a diversity of spiritual manifestations that allows Pentecostals to be welcoming to the Spirit's work in a variety of ways that is controlled by the Spirit. The Holy Spirit empowers the church with spiritual gifts to aid it in fulfilling its divine mandate to "make disciples of all nations" (Matt 28:19).

A PENTECOSTAL PERSPECTIVE

Pentecostal spirituality has, since its inception, upheld the basic orthodox doctrines and tenets of the faith. The major point of distinction is that the Pentecostal believes in Spirit baptism as evidenced by speaking in tongues and that God continues to work in the church through supernatural means. The early Pentecostals were accused of being demonic, deranged, gullible, and troublesome. Those making these charges usually did so based on Pentecostals' belief and practice of spiritual gifts.[7]

However, any attempts to publicly humiliate Pentecostals into denying their beliefs were futile. Instead, backed by their reading of Scripture and their experience in the Spirit, Pentecostals boldly stood their ground. Because of this, the affirmation of Pentecostals that spiritual gifts are given by the Holy Spirit and are the normative working of the Spirit within the contemporary church is a central contribution that the movement has made to the history of Christianity.[8] This is no small contribution but a restoration of the church back to the biblical pattern of experiencing the Spirit's moving within the fellowship of believers.

A Pentecostal view of spiritual gifts highlights their significance in empowering and transforming the worshipping community of believers. As people who seek for a powerful experience with the Spirit, Pentecostals eagerly desire the manifestation of the Spirit's gifts. This yearning for spiritual manifestations is rooted in the apostle Paul's admonition for the Corinthian's to "desire earnestly spiritual gifts" (1 Cor 12:31). To this point, Pentecostal scholar Tony Richie writes,

> Based on a straight-forward approach to the Bible, Pentecostals are continuationists, affirming that New Testament spiritual gifts continue to be active today wherever believers yield in humble obedience to the Holy Spirit's gracious working.[9]

7. Land, *Pentecostal Spirituality*, 159.

8. Kärkkäinen, *Pneumatology*, 101.

9. Richie, *Saved, Delivered, and Healed.*

For the Pentecostal, the aspiration for spiritual manifestations to be present in the church is about more than the mere occurrence of novel activity. Instead, the Pentecostal longs for spiritual manifestations because they view their activity as being something that displays the presence of God in their presence. It is this longing for the invisible Spirit to reveal Himself in visible ways that underlies the Pentecostal's emphasis on spiritual manifestations.

Pentecostal spirituality emphasizes the expectation of the supernatural to invade the natural world. This expectation goes beyond the events of a worship service and into daily life. In discussing the Pentecostal's perspective on the matter, Matthias Wenk writes,

> Three major theological themes surface regarding Pentecostal perceptions of how spiritual gifts manifest the in-braking of the kingdom of God into this world: the glory of God (or the doxological orientation of spiritual gifts), the power of God (or the ministerial orientation toward empowerment), and the justice of God (or the transformational orientation of spiritual gifts).[10]

Such a framework reveals that the Pentecostal can integrate spiritual gifts into their outlook of worship, philosophy of ministry, and view of end-time hope. While the Pentecostal church does not always live up to the ideal, when the diversity of spiritual gifts operates as God designed, the Pentecostal church becomes a visible representation of the community of the Spirit. In order for this to occur, the Pentecostal church must take seriously Paul's instruction to desire spiritual gifts as they "pursue love" (1 Cor 14:1). Since a focus on spiritual gifts could lead to a false sense of elitism or to the neglect of other aspects of the faith, Pentecostals must be careful to insist both on the importance of the fruits of the Spirit (as recorded in Galatians 5:22–24) and on seeking after the Giver of the gifts, the Holy Spirit, rather than after the gifts themselves.

Pentecostal spirituality emphasizes the expectation of the supernatural to invade the natural world.

10. Wenk, "Spiritual Gifts," 302.

However, while most Pentecostals today believe that the whole range of biblical gifts continues today, some have ceased in their practice of these manifestations. In fact, many churches that in principle allow the gifts of the Spirit to operate within their public worship are practically cessationsist in their stifling of any manifestations that do not fit their traditional order of service.[11] This disconnect between doctrinal belief and practical behavior is one that cannot be sustained for long. Eventually, either the behavior of the congregation will line back up with their doctrinal beliefs or they will change their doctrinal beliefs to line up with their current behavior. For the Pentecostal congregations who are currently living in a disconnect between belief and behavior, they run the real danger of losing the distinctive contribution of Pentecostalism (spiritual gifts are for today). When a Pentecostal church fails to practice spiritual manifestations, not only does the church lose all the blessings and empowerment provided by the Spirit through these gifts, but they also lose something of their identity.[12]

The modern Pentecostal church is wise to continue its tradition of encouraging its adherents to "desire earnestly spiritual gifts" (1 Cor 14:1). Since spiritual gifts originate from the Spirit and are "distributed to each one individually just as He wills" (1 Cor 12:11), every Spirit-empowered Pentecostal has a responsibility to operate within their spiritual giftings in order that the ministry of the church might be effective in this present age.

CONCLUSION

The operation of spiritual manifestations is an essential aspect of the life of the church, for they reveal the work of the Holy Spirit in the physical realm, making the invisible God visible to believers. These gifts of grace are not given as a reward for good behavior, but as God wills. Therefore, spiritual gifts are not for personal edification or self-promotion, but for the benefit of the entire community of believers. When used with the intent of building up the church, spiritual gifts can be a powerful tool for fulfilling the church's divine mission of glorifying Christ and evangelizing the lost.

Pentecostal spirituality is known for its belief in the continuance of spiritual manifestations within the church today. Pentecostals have remained steadfast in their belief that spiritual gifts are an expected component of the church's experience and come from the Holy Spirit. In this way,

11. Keener, *Spirit Hermeneutics*, 8.

12. Richie, *Essential of Pentecostal Theology*, 46.

the desire for spiritual manifestations comes from the biblical exhortation to earnestly desire spiritual gifts, and Pentecostals view these manifestations as signs of God's presence in their midst.

APPLICATION QUESTIONS

1. What spiritual gifts might the Spirit want you to use to help build up your church?

2. How can we use our spiritual gifts to support and encourage others, even those who may have different gifts than our own?

FURTHER READING

Bruner, Frederick Dale. *A Theology of the Holy Spirit: The Pentecostal Experience and the New Testament Witness*. Eugene, OR: Wipf & Stock, 1997.

Chan, Simon. *Pentecostal theology and the Christian Spiritual Tradition*. London: A&C Black, 2000.

Jacobsen, Douglas. *Thinking in the Spirit: Theologies of the Early Pentecostal Movement*. Bloomington: Indiana University Press, 2003.

Kydd, Ronald A. N. *Charismatic Gifts in the Early Church: The Gifts of the Spirit in the First 300 Years*. Peabody, MA: Hendrickson, 2015.

Storms, Sam. *Understanding Spiritual Gifts: A Comprehensive Guide*. Grand Rapids: Zondervan, 2020.

Stronstad, Roger. *Spirit, Scripture, and Theology: A Pentecostal Perspective*. Eugene, OR: Wipf & Stock, 2019.

11

Perspectives on Miracles

It is in the signs and wonders—understood as miracles of healing and the casting out of demons—that Pentecostal and charismatic Christianity has made its most significant impact.

—ALLAN ANDERSON

INTRODUCTION

I will never forget the miraculous event that took place on one of my trips to Africa. After I had finished preaching a sermon about the results of believing the gospel, a young mother brought her son up and asked,

> "Preacher, do you believe that the God you talked about is able to heal my son?"
>
> Noticing the look of anguish in the eyes of this young mother, I glanced down at the child and it was painfully obvious that the boy could not see. Turning to this heartbroken African mother, I asked, "What happened to your son?"
>
> With a tone of hopeless desperation the woman replied, "My son was born blind and I have no way to help him."
>
> My heart was immediately broken for this poor mother. I could tell that she wanted to believe in God's power, but she was not totally convinced it was possible. I remember saying something like, "Yes, I believe that my God can heal your child. Can I pray for him?"
>
> "Yes, please do!" She said with the slightest hint of hope.

> After announcing this need to a few other ministers that were gathered nearby, we began to lay our hands on this young boy's eyes and pray for the faith of this mother to bring the miracle-working power of God.
>
> What happened next I can only describe as a miracle. The young child's eyes began to clear and he was suddenly able to focus on objects around the church. In wonder the boy looked around until his eyes stopped on his mother's face. The moment the two of them locked eyes was one of the most beautiful things I have ever witnessed.

The miracle that happened that night cannot be explained through natural means. There is no scientific or natural explanation for how that young boy went from a state of complete blindness to having perfect vision. The only logical explanation that can justify what happened is that God performed a miracle.

Yet within modern secular philosophy the idea of divine miracles is seen as a misguided exaggeration of the religious naïve. The famous philosopher David Hume maintained that it is impossible in principle to prove that a miracle has occurred, and the only miracle is that anyone could be stupid enough to believe in Christianity. Those who agree with Hume believe that any support for the existence of a miracle, even if it is provided by the strongest conceivable testimony, will always be outweighed by the evidence that the laws of nature have not been violated. In other words, there can be no evidence presented for a miracle that can trump the evidence that a miracle has not occurred.

While, admittedly, miracles are uncommon—and, by definition, they certainly exist outside the realm of normal human experience—this does not mean they are impossible. The question must be asked, how many miracles would it take to disprove Hume's theory that miracles are impossible? The answer is obviously only one. Further, Hume's argument against miracles is built on the presumption of the absolute regularity of nature. While God certainly created an ordered universe that is governed by natural laws, as the Creator of physical laws, God is not bound by the laws He created. Therefore, from a Christian perspective, not only is it logical to believe in miracles, but they carry a theological message of God's interaction with humanity. For the Christian, miracles are manifestations of God's compassion, power, and desire to work within humanity. In short, miracles testify to a personal God who interacts with His creation.

CREATED ORDER

God has created a world of order. The Designer has constructed the universe in such a way that it functions within consistent laws of nature. The beauty, complexity, and fine-tuning of the natural world all declare "the work of His hands" (Ps 19:1). When God spoke, "Let there be" (Gen 1:3, 6, 14), the command of the eternal Word birthed physical reality *ex nihilo* (out of nothing). Responding to the sovereign command of an omnipotent (all-powerful) God, the natural world was ordered and established.

The constructing of the laws of nature not only reveals God's "invisible attributes, His eternal power and divine nature" (Rom 1:20), but it also allows for the continuation of human life. If the laws of nature were unpredictable and continually changing, the flourishing of human life and scientific understanding would be impossible. However, God established the natural order of the universe with laws that govern its function. These natural laws are God-ordained and declared by Him to be "good" (Gen 1:4, 10, 12, 18, 21, 25). As such, God would actually be working against divine faithfulness and His own creation if miracles were to become normal, everyday events. Such a world would look very much like *Alice in Wonderland*, in which unpredictability is the only thing one can predict.

While an *Alice in Wonderland* world may be a fun fantasy to read about, it would be a horrible reality to live in. The constant chaos and changeable nature of that kind of world would make life impossible. If the laws of physics where constantly shifting, human life could not survive. Such an existence might be expected if there was no Creator, and the cosmos came to be through truly random chance. However, it is through the consistent physical laws of God's ordered world that divine faithfulness is demonstrated to humanity.[1] In this way, God's divine faithfulness *is* the foundation upon which everything within creation is built for the "builder of all things is God" (Heb 3:4). Through the created order of physical laws, God's divine faithfulness is demonstrated, and humanity is able to function and flourish as we live within God's created order.

Throughout church history, the most common definition of a miracle has been a divine action that transcends or contradicts the ordinary laws of nature.[2] A miracle is an event of which explanation is owed to a special divine action. The term "miracle" is often thrown around in such a loose

---

1. Polkinghorne, *Science and Providence*, 61.
2. Keener, *Miracles Today*, 3.

way that the word has lost some of its meaning. Often people refer to an unexpected outcome, a scientific breakthrough, or even the birth of a child as a "miracle." When they use the word in this context, what they really mean is that the event is special. Without question, the birth of a child is special, but in the proper use of the term it is not a "miracle." The birth of a child happens hundreds of thousands of times every single day. The event of a newborn, while special, is not something that contradicts the ordinary laws of nature. A baby born of a virgin, however, is something altogether different. That is a miracle.

Additionally, although we may not understand the science behind some medical breakthroughs that bring healing to a disease, this lack of knowledge does not constitute a suspension of the natural laws of physics. For instance, someone who goes through immunotherapy for cancer and their body responds in a positive way has not experienced a miracle that transcends natural laws; instead, they are blessed to receive the benefits of scientific advancements in cancer treatments. Whereas, when someone who has been blind from birth—without the aid of any medical procedure—is suddenly is able to see again, that is a suspension of the ordinary laws of nature and, by definition, a miracle.

A few years ago, I was in a church service where a woman who was completely deaf in one ear was miraculously healed. This woman had gone to numerous doctors who tested her ability to hear and told her that she had zero hearing in her right ear. However, after the sermon she came down to the front of the church to pray. Suddenly, from the silent reverence of prayer, she let out an excited shout. She began to loudly proclaim, "Glory to God! Hallelujah! Thank you, Jesus!" After a few minutes of joyous worship, she stopped and asked if she could share what just happened. Taking the microphone, she explained what the doctors had told her about the severity of her earing condition, but she testified that God had just healed her deaf ear. Suddenly, she could hear perfectly out of her previously deaf ear. Not long after that night, this lady went back to the doctor and was able to pass a hearing test in her right ear. Such an event cannot be explained in terms of natural laws or processes.

NEW TESTAMENT MIRACLES

A biblical framework for defining an act as a miracle includes three important features. First, the miracle is a *temporary* exception to the natural order. The raising of Lazarus from the dead was a temporary suspension of the natural order. This is not the normal way death functions. Dead men normally stay dead. Second, it is an *exception* to the ordinary course of nature. In other words, we should not expect resurrections to happen at every funeral. Thirdly, miracles *originate* from a divine source. Wonderous acts that originate from human sources should not be classified as miracles. Finally, the *purpose* of divine miracles is to reveal the glory of God.[3]

Why is this framework important? First, as we will shortly see, one of the primary purposes of miracles is to demonstrate to the unbeliever the glory of God. Therefore, if the Christian is constantly attributing as divinely orchestrated miracles that for which the unbeliever can easily and justifiably point to natural causes, the testimony of the Christian is greatly damaged. Secondly, the hard reality is that everyone who prays for a miracle does not receive the answer they desire. More often than not, God chooses to not suspend the normal and ordinary laws of nature. However, miracles play an important role in the New Testament, validating the apostles' gospel preaching and demonstrating God's love and compassion for the hurting.

Additionally, they attest to Jesus' divinity. Jesus' miracles demonstrate that he is the divine Son of God and not merely a good moral teacher. This aspect of miracles is emphasized in the Gospel of John, which refers to them as "signs" (John 2:11; 4:54; 20:30–31). The New Testament writers are quick to record the miracles surrounding the life and ministry of Jesus Christ. From a miraculous conception to walking on water, the Son of God demonstrated divine power. The New Testament records over twenty miracles of healing performed by Jesus and nine accounts in which Christ demonstrated power over natural laws. The miracle acts of Jesus range from walking on water to raising the dead and everything in between. These miracles were a manifestation of God's kingdom breaking forth in the person of Jesus Christ. Jesus' miracles demonstrated that the kingdom of God had invaded the darkness of this world, bringing healing, liberation, and restoration. Throughout the New Testament, the healings performed by Christ are about more than just the physical restoration of the sick, but they also serve as a symbol of the ultimate restoration that will occur in the end times. In a very real sense, every miracle Jesus accomplished served as a foretaste of that which is to come in our future age when Christ returns and re-creation is complete in fulfillment of God's promise, "Behold, I am making all things new" (Rev 21:5).

3. Purtill, "Defining Miracles," 64.

Furthermore, New Testament miracles served as an effective tool to validate the message of the apostles. To authenticate their preaching and demonstrate that they were empowered by the Holy Spirit, the apostles performed numerous miracles, including healings, exorcisms, and wonders of nature. Following the day of Pentecost, "a sense of awe; and many wonders and signs were taking place through the apostles" (Acts 2:43), resulting in a multitude of conversions and the continual growth of the church as God "adding to their number day by day those who were being saved" (Acts 2:47). From a New Testament perspective, miracles are never meant to be ends in themselves. Instead, the purpose of miracles is to demonstrate the power of God. Through revealing God's power, the working of miracles builds the faith of the Christian and leads the unsaved toward faith in Jesus Christ.

From a New Testament perspective, miracles are never meant to be ends in themselves. Instead, the purpose of miracles is to demonstrate the power of God. Through revealing God's power, the working of miracles builds the faith of the Christian and leads the unsaved toward faith in Jesus Christ.

Finally, miracles serve as a witness to God's compassion and love for suffering humanity. The miracles of Jesus and the apostles not only demonstrate God's power, but they reveal God's gracious character. The healing of the leper (Mark 1:40–45), the feeding of the five thousand (Matt 14:13–21), the raising of the widow's son (Lk 7:11–17), the healing of the woman with a bleeding disorder (Mark 5:25–34), and countless other accounts all illustrate God's compassionate heart for the hurting. In every miracle performed in the New Testament, God is revealed to be someone who sees, cares about, and responds to human suffering. The biblical position on miracles cannot help but expose the Christian God as a God who is not remote or indifferent, but intimately involved in his people's struggles. The biblical testimony demonstrates that God's compassion extends to all people, regardless of their social standing or the severity of their suffering. In summary, the miracles of the New Testament provide the reader with evidence of God's compassion for the suffering and his desire to restore wholeness to broken lives.

A PENTECOSTAL PERSPECTIVE

For many Pentecostals, the experience or witnessing of miracles distinguishes Pentecostals from other Christians. In many ways, familiarity with the miraculous is a central element that connects Pentecostals with the early church.[4] For Pentecostals, the belief that God can miraculously intervene in human affairs is foundational to their understanding of God's nature. They expect such divine action to occur and testify of God's miracle-working power in their preaching and evangelism. To this point, Pentecostal scholar Kimberly Alexander states,

> From its inception, the Pentecostal movement has preached a gospel which includes healing for the whole person. Healing miracles were expected and the demonstrations of God's power to heal became the "drawing cards" for many missionary and evangelistic efforts. The testimonies which arose in the Pentecostal community, and circulated in the wider geographic community, were in most cases the "word of mouth" advertising which was utilized by the growing movement.[5]

Such an expectation and witness of the miracle-working power of God proved to be an effective tool for spreading the gospel and aided the unprecedented growth of Pentecostalism. From a Pentecostal reading of Scripture, the miraculous events found within the Bible are a testimony not only of God's miracle-working in the past, but of His ability to perform the miraculous today. As such, Pentecostals believe that Jesus' miracles were manifestations of his divine power and authority as opposed to merely symbolic acts of compassion.

From their reading of the numerous accounts of miracles in the book of Acts, Pentecostals view miracles as not limited to the past but possible in the present. Empowered by the same Holy Spirit whom Jesus promised to send after his departure, Pentecostals look for the same miraculous demonstrations performed in the early church. The Pentecostal sees the signs and wonders of the Acts of the Apostles as cosmic signs that testify of a divine pouring "forth of My Spirit on all" (Acts 2:17). As people of the last days (the period between the first and second coming of Jesus), Pentecostals believe that the same miraculous works that played such a vital role in the early church are still relevant today. In fact, the explosion of the global

---

4. Vondey, *Pentecostal Theology*, 107.

5. Alexander, *Pentecostal Healing*, 2.

Pentecostal movement can be credited in large part to its emphasis on supernatural miracles.

Pentecostals believe that miracles are an expected (although not routine) component of the Christian life. Since the Christian worships and is filled with the presence of God, they can expect divine miracles to happen, "for I, the Lord, am your healer" (Exod 15:26). In Pentecostal worship services, prayer is made for healing, deliverance, and other miracles. These prayers may be accompanied by the laying on of hands, anointing with oil, or other outward manifestations of faith (Jas 5:14–15). Within the context of a worship service, Pentecostals believe that miracles are for the edification and strengthening of the whole church, not just the individual who receives them. The performing of miracles, like all other Spirit-given gifts, is designed to build up the church's faith. Additionally, Pentecostals believe that miracles occur outside the context of the church and are not limited to Christian worship gatherings. The very same God who demonstrates divine powers in sacred worship services is also capable of performing miracles within everyday life, such as a miraculous healing, supernatural provision of resources, and divine intervention in a crisis.

> **Empowered by the same Holy Spirit whom Jesus promised to send after his departure, Pentecostals look for the same miraculous demonstrations performed in the early church.**

Like the New Testament apostles, the early Pentecostals often appealed to the manifestation of miracles as validation of their message. Just as signs and wonders were an important part of confirming the message of the early church, the early Pentecostals viewed the presence of signs and wonders as validation of their Spirit-filled witness.[6] For Pentecostals, the accompanying of the miraculous is the fulfillment of Jesus' promise that "these signs will accompany those who have believed" (Mark 16:17). These miracles are expected not just as a validating sign of God's power and presence but also as a means of evangelism and spreading the gospel message. In this way, the Pentecostal views miracles as part of the church's witness to this world.

6. Archer, *Gospel Revisited*, 30.

This means that the Pentecostal should not seek for miracles simply for the sake of sensationalist curiosity or to satisfy a desire for the shocking or unusual. Instead, they are testimonies of God's gracious presence bursting into the normal order. Such breaking forth of divine miracles points to the wonderous glory of God and ought to humble humanity as they recognize that such acts can never be accounted for by human work or power.[7]

Like all manifestations of the Spirit, God's miraculous acts within the church are about much more than those who directly benefit. This means that the ultimate purpose of God's miraculous actions should not be limited to those who receive divine intervention. Instead, the working of miracles is designed to build up the faith of the entire church and to serve as a witness to the unbeliever of God's power and authority. Pentecostal scholar Tony Richie has observed,

> Currently, much of Third World Christianity is Pentecostal in nature precisely through the supernatural or miraculous aspects of Pentecostal Christianity. Not surprisingly, Pentecostals connect effective evangelism and extraordinary missionary success to occurrences of such signs and wonders.[8]

For the Pentecostal, not only are miracles an evangelistic witness of God's power, but they are a divine foretaste of the future state of the Christian. Miracles are about more than merely God intruding on the natural order of this world, but they speak to our future hope of new creation, where God will make "all things new" (Rev 21:5).

CONCLUSION

As the Creator of the universe, God has crafted an orderly universe governed by natural laws. These laws not only reveal God's divine attributes but are also crucial for human life's existence and scientific understanding. Yet, as Creator, God is not confined by natural laws or prevented from working outside of them. Therefore, the Christian can believe the miraculous accounts found within Scripture and testify to the miracle-working power of God.

By confirm Jesus' divinity, miracles validate Christ's claim to be the Son of God. They demonstrate His authority over creation, His ability to heal the sick, raise the dead, calm storms, and even multiply food. By

7. Macchia, *Tongues of Fire*, 235.

8. Richie, *Essentials of Pentecostal Theology*, 72.

witnessing these miraculous acts, people were led to recognize Jesus as more than a mere human teacher or prophet. Miracles also validate the apostles' preaching, providing tangible evidence of the truth they proclaimed. The book of Acts records numerous instances where the apostles performed miracles, such as healing the sick, casting out demons, and raising the dead. These miracles served as visible demonstrations of divine authority and empowered their words with credibility. By witnessing these miracles, the lost were not only amazed but also compelled to hear the message being preached. Additionally, miracles demonstrate God's deep compassion for humanity, revealing His desire to bring healing, restoration, and liberation to a broken world. Through every miraculous action, a divine response is made to human suffering with love and mercy. These miraculous acts of compassion demonstrate God's desire to alleviate human pain and restore wholeness.

For Pentecostals, miracles form a fundamental part of their faith. The accounts of miracles in Scripture are more than historical accounts; for the Pentecostal, they serve as inspirational stories that build faith that God to do the miraculous in our present age. The Pentecostal sees the performance of miracles as instrumental in building the faith of the Christian and as a form of convincing the skeptic of the reality of God.

APPLICATION QUESTIONS

1. Have you ever experienced a miracle? If so, what happened?

2. How do miracles provide Christians with a divine foretaste of our eternal future?

FURTHER READING

Alexander, Kimberly. *Pentecostal Healing: Models in Theology and Practice*. Leiden: Brill, 2019.

Clark, Randy. *Eyewitness to Miracles: Watching the Gospel Come to Life*. Nashville: Thomas Nelson, 2018.

Keener, Craig S. *Miracles: The Credibility of the New Testament Accounts.* 2 vols. Grand Rapids: Baker, 2011.

———. *Miracles Today: The Supernatural Work of God in the Modern World.* Grand Rapids: Baker, 2021.

McGee, Gary B. *Miracles, Missions, and American Pentecostalism.* Maryknoll, NY: Orbis, 2010.

Smith, James K. A., and Amos Yong, eds. *Science and the Spirit: A Pentecostal Engagement with the Sciences.* Bloomington: Indiana University Press, 2010.

Yong, Amos. *The Spirit Poured Out on All Flesh: Pentecostalism and the Possibility of Global Theology.* Grand Rapids: Baker Academic, 2005.

12

Perspectives on Future Hope

God is the last thing.
—Steven J. Land

INTRODUCTION

In the hands of a master painter, a canvas is a sacred space, a playground of creativity and expression. Imagine a lush landscape with dense forests, majestic mountains, and rivers running deep and clear, reflecting the colors of a vibrant, setting sun. Every detail and every stroke of the paintbrush is a testament to the artist's understanding of nature and deep love for creation.

But then, in the blink of an eye, the painting falls from its canvas and lands in a paint can. Colors blend into an undecipherable mess, marring the once-pristine landscape and turning the masterpiece into an ugly ruin. The masterpiece, it seems, is destroyed. However, the artist, the creator of this landscape, does not throw away the canvas in dismay. There is a calmness in his eyes, an unspoken assurance. He sees not an end but a beginning. He looks beyond the ruin and sees an opportunity. In the mess, he sees potential and a chance for redemption.

With a renewed resolve, the artist sets to work. The room is silent except for the gentle whispers of the painter's brush against the canvas. Slowly and purposefully, he works to redeem the stained painting. The strokes are confident and unerring. Where once there was a splotch of paint, now there blooms a beautiful tree, its branches reaching toward the heavens, clothed in leaves of every color imaginable. The mess has not been erased; instead, it has been transformed. The landscape is different now—not as it was, but stunning in its own unique way. The fall has been transformed into a purposeful part of the artwork, integrated into the landscape to enhance its beauty, depth, and story. What was once a symbol of disaster is now a testament to grace, to redemption, and to the creative power of the master artist. The artist has demonstrated that nothing is beyond repair and that there is always hope for renewal and transformation, even in the face of ruin.

Like the master artist in the illustration, God has taken the ruined painting of this current world, which has been marred by sin, suffering, and death, and redeemed it. While this restoration has begun through the work of Christ, it is not finished. The future hope of the Christian is the ultimate restoration of creation through a new heaven and new earth. This new creation is not just a restoration of the old but a complete re-creation that surpasses the original in beauty and perfection.

Eschatology, the study of the end times and the ultimate fate of humanity and the world, is a vital and profound part of Christian theology. By exploring eschatological topics, believers gain an understanding of significant topics such as death, judgment, heaven, hell, the second coming of Christ, the resurrection of the dead, and the final state of the cosmos. Within eschatology, the Christian reflects on their existential purpose and the culmination of their faith.

OUR PRESENT HOPE

While Christian eschatology is a complex and often debated topic, it has important practical implications for Christian living and mission. First and foremost, it reminds the Christian of God's ultimate purpose for redeeming humanity—to be in union with God in a new heaven and earth. This hope gives meaning and purpose to the struggles and challenges of this life, and encourages believers to persevere in faith, hope, and love. At the same time, eschatology helps Christians to avoid the pitfalls of utopianism or despair. While Christians are called to work for the kingdom of God, they also recognize that the fullness of the kingdom will only be realized when the King returns. This means that they place their ultimate hope not in human progress or achievement, but in the promise of God's grace and mercy.

Any approach to New Testament theology that considers eschatology to be a minor point of focus must seriously reevaluate its reading of

Scripture, for the whole story of the Bible is designed to point the reader toward an eschatological hope. As Anthony Hoekema puts it,

> The nature of New Testament eschatology may be summed up under three observations: (1) the great eschatological event predicted in the Old Testament has happened; (2) what the Old Testament writers seemed to depict as one movement is now seen to involve two stages: the present age and the age of the future; and (3) the relation between these two eschatological stages is that the blessings of the present eschatological age are the pledge and guarantee of greater blessings to come.[1]

This present hope centers around the future return of Christ as the catalyst moment that the Christian ought to be looking toward. Christians ought to eagerly awaiting the second coming of Jesus Christ, who will usher in the final realization of God's plan for creation. The promise of Jesus' return is repeatedly taught throughout the New Testament and throughout church history and continues to be a central article of faith within Christian theology. Before Christ's ascension Jesus assured his followers that even though he was leaving them, he would ultimately return (Matt 24–25; John 14–17; Acts 1:10–11). As part of this, Christian eschatology has historically emphasized the imminence of Christ's return and the need for vigilance and readiness.

Examination of eschatological topics aids believers in appreciating the significance of Christ's return and the restoration and renewal of all things. This expectation motivates Christians to live in accordance with Christ's teachings, actively participating in God's redemptive work and proclaiming the good news of salvation to all. This understanding equips believers to navigate the complexities of life with purpose, hope, and an eternal perspective, as they endeavor to live in accordance with God's ultimate plan for humanity and the universe. G. K.

Any approach to New Testament theology that considers eschatology to be a minor point of focus must seriously reevaluate its reading of Scripture.

---

1. Hoekema, *Bible and the Future*, 21.

Beale reminds us that our present hope is secure in God's faithful actions in the past:

> Christians live between "D-day" and "V-Day." D-day was the first coming of Christ, when the opponent was defeated decisively; V-day is the final coming of Christ, at which time the adversary will finally and completely surrender. The hope of the final victory is so much more vivid because of the unshakably firm conviction that the battle that decides the victory has already taken place.[2]

As Christians, our eschatological beliefs should not only shape our personal faith and spiritual practices, but also inform our engagement with the world around us. In a world plagued by injustice, inequality, and violence, Christians have a responsibility to work for the common good and to bear witness to the truth of the gospel. This means speaking out against systems of oppression, advocating for the marginalized, and working to create a more just and equitable society, while continually in acts of compassion, seeking to alleviate suffering and poverty, and speaking out against injustice and oppression. Doing so while continually bearing witness to the truth of the gospel and inviting others to join in the hope and joy of the kingdom.

At the same time, the Christian's eschatological beliefs should provide a sense of humility and perspective. While the disciple of Christ works for the kingdom of God, the Christian must recognize that their efforts are not what cause God's kingdom to advance, or the ultimate fulfillment of God's promises come to pass. As such, we do not give in to despair or hopelessness in the face of hardship and suffering but continue to place our confidence in God's ability to accomplish His divine purposes.

Motivated by a confidence that God's agendas will come to pass, the Christian should be inspired by their eschatology to continually deepen their relationship with God and cultivate a posture of spiritual readiness. Just as a bride waits in excited anticipation for her groom, the follower of Christ awaits the coming of Christ with joy and hope. The Christian ought to live in prepared expectation for Christ's imminent return and echo the pray of John the Revelator, "Come, Lord Jesus" (Rev 22:20).

2. Beale, *Union with the Resurrected Christ*, 62.

A PENTECOSTAL PERSPECTIVE

From a Pentecostal perspective, eschatology is of paramount importance for both theology and identity. Without a doubt, issues surrounding the end times did not play a secondary role in the rise of Pentecostalism.[3] In the very initial development of Pentecostalism, a significant emphasis was put on the second coming of Jesus Christ. The conviction that the triumphant return of Jesus Christ as "King of Kings and Lord of Lords" (Rev 19:6) is imminent (at any moment) is central to Pentecostal theology and serves as an articulation of the movement's core hope for the end of time.[4]

Central to a Pentecostal eschatology is the role of the Holy Spirit. Through the power of the resurrected Christ, the Christian's eschatological hope of resurrection is inevitable, for "Christ has been raised from the dead, the first fruits of those who are asleep" (1 Cor 15:20). While the Christian's future hope is inevitable, it will not be fully realized until Christ's return, for "then comes the end, when He hands over the kingdom to the God and Father, when He has abolished all rule and all authority and power" (1 Cor 15:24). In summarizing the Spirit's role in the already/not yet tension of our future hope, Gordon Fee writes,

> The whole of Paul's understanding of our present life in the Spirit, paradoxical as it may seem at times, is put into proper perspective if we begin by realizing that the Spirit is both the fulfillment of the eschatological promises of God and the down payment on our certain future. We are both already and not yet. The Spirit is the evidence of the one, the guarantee of the other.[5]

While our eschatological future has begun in our present—as evidenced by the presence of God's empowering Spirit—until the consummation of our future hope, God has provided us with the Spirit's empowerment to aid the church to fulfill its end-time mission in this present age.

Historically, Pentecostal eschatology has also fostered a strong commitment to holiness and sanctification. Driven by a sense of the imminent return of Christ, the spiritual lifestyle of the Pentecostal has been characterized by prayer, fasting, and an emphasis on living righteously. Through repeated sermons and teaching about the future judgment, the Pentecostal adherent is continually encouraged to live in a godly manner. Consequently,

3. Faupel, *Everlasting Gospel*, 20.

4. Althouse, "Eschatology," 268.

5. Fee, *God's Empowering Presence*, 826.

the lifestyle of Pentecostals is often marked by abstaining from ungodly practices or evil associations. It must not be forgotten that such a lifestyle is a direct result of their eschatological beliefs. In short, Pentecostal eschatology encourages believers to live a life of holiness and dedication to God in preparation for the second coming of Christ. This includes abstaining from sin and pursuing righteousness, as well as seeking the guidance and empowerment of the Holy Spirit in all aspects of life.

From a Pentecostal perspective, eschatology is about more than apocalyptic destruction and the "end of the world," but it focuses on the work of the Holy Spirit to defeat "the spiritual forces of wickedness" (Eph 2:12) and the antichrist spirit that is "already in the world" (1 John 4:3). A Pentecostal eschatology is incomplete without appreciating the fact that the Pentecostal views the Holy Spirit as playing a critical role in empowering believers to perform signs and wonders, prophesy, push back satanic agendas, and carry out the work of evangelism until Jesus Christ returns.

In outlining a classical Pentecostal approach to eschatology, Pentecostal scholar Tony Richie writes,

> Traditionally Pentecostal have adhered to a premillennial eschatology maintaining that the second coming of Christ will precede and prepare the way for a literal one thousand-year reign of Christ on earth. For the most part that has meant belief in a pre-tribulation "rapture" (catching away) of the church to meet the Lord in the air (1 Thess 4:16–17), followed by seven years of unprecedented tribulation on earth (Matt 24:21) before the actual coming of Christ to earth (Heb 9:28), and then the millennium (Rev 20:1–6), itself followed by the judgment of the present age and establishment of the new creation (Rev 20:7—21:1).[6]

The belief in the imminent return of Jesus Christ has led Pentecostals to live in constant anticipation of the end times, which in turn governs their behaviors and attitudes. The expectation of Christ's return inspires an attitude of watchfulness and spiritual readiness, acting as a moral compass that guides Pentecostals' actions and decisions. This sense of imminence instills a strong sense of urgency in evangelism and mission work, inspiring Pentecostals to spread the gospel message, knowing that Jesus promises, "This gospel of the kingdom shall be preached in the whole world as a testimony to all the nations, and then the end will come" (Matt 24:14).

---

6. Richie, *Essential of Pentecostal Theology*, 163.

Pentecostals are also uniquely positioned to engage in acts of compassion. Our emphasis on the gifts and fruit of the Spirit encourages us to act with kindness, gentleness, and self-control, and to seek to alleviate suffering and poverty wherever we find it. This is a manifestation of the Spirit's work in us and through us, and a powerful testimony to the love of God.

The Pentecostal believes in the active and transformative power of the Holy Spirit in our lives and in the world. The Spirit not only convicts and comforts, but also propels us to action, empowering us to be agents of eschatological change. The anticipation of a future divine kingdom offers hope and resilience in the face of adversity. It provides a framework for understanding and coping with suffering, seeing it as temporary and in the context of eternal life. This future-oriented perspective can be a source of comfort and strength in difficult times and motives the Pentecostal toward compassionate ministry.

> **The belief in the imminent return of Jesus Christ has led Pentecostals to live in constant anticipation of the end times, which in turn governs their behaviors and attitudes.**

CONCLUSION

Pentecostal eschatology offers a unique perspective on the end times that is based on a deep understanding of the power of the Holy Spirit and the ongoing work of the church. The urgency of the end times also motivates Pentecostals to share the gospel and bring others into a saving relationship with Jesus Christ. While there is much debate about the details of the end times, Pentecostals are united in their belief in the imminent return of Jesus Christ and the power of the Holy Spirit to guide and empower the church until Christ returns. As we look to the future and the coming of Jesus Christ, let us be filled with hope and joy, knowing that the Holy Spirit is with us and that we have a vital role to play in carrying out the work of the kingdom of God.

In conclusion, from a Pentecostal perspective eschatology is not merely a set of abstract doctrines about the end times, but it has profound practical implications on Pentecostals' faith and way of life. It shapes their attitudes, behaviors, and responses to the world around them, influencing their spiritual practices, ethical decisions, and sense of mission. It provides a theological framework for understanding suffering and offers hope for a divine future.

APPLICATION QUESTIONS

1. In what ways is eschatology central to Pentecostal faith and practice?

2. How might rejecting a belief in the imminent return of Jesus Christ influence the future of Pentecostalism?

FURTHER READING

Althouse, Peter, and Rob Waddell. *Perspectives in Pentecostal Eschatologies: World without End*. Cambridge: James Clarke, 2012.

Faupel, D William. *The Everlasting Gospel: The Significance of Eschatology in the Development of Pentecostal Thought*. Leiden: Brill, 2019.

Land, Steven Jack. *Pentecostal Spirituality: A Passion for the Kingdom*. London: A&C Black, 1993.

McQueen, Larry. *Towards a Pentecostal Eschatology: Discerning the Way Forward*. Leiden: Brill, 2019.

Thompson, Matthew K. *Kingdom Come: Revisioning Pentecostal Eschatology*. Leiden: Brill, 2019.

Bibliography

Alexander, Kimberly E. *Pentecostal Healing: Models in Theology and Practice.* Blandford Forum, UK: Deo, 2013.

Althouse, Peter. *Spirit of the Last Days: Pentecostal Eschatology in Conversation with Jürgen Moltmann.* London: A&C Black, 2003.

———. "Eschatology: The Always Present Hope." In *The Routledge Handbook of Pentecostal Theology*, edited by Wolfgang Vondey, 268–78. London: Routledge, 2020.

Anderson, Allan Heaton. *An Introduction to Pentecostalism: Global Charismatic Christianity.* 2nd ed. Cambridge: Cambridge University Press, 2013.

———. "Towards a Pentecostal Missiology for the Majority World." In *Azusa Street and Beyond*, edited by G. McClung, 169–90. 2nd ed. Alachua, FL: Bridge-Logos, 2006.

Anderson, Tawa J., W. Michael Clark, and David K. Naugle. *An Introduction to Christian Worldview: Pursuing God's Perspective in a Pluralistic World.* Downers Grove, IL: InterVarsity, 2017.

Archer, Kenneth J. *The Gospel Revisited: Towards a Pentecostal Theology of Worship and Witness.* Eugene, OR: Pickwick 2011.

Arrington, French L. "The Use of the Bible by Pentecostals." *Pneuma* 16.1 (1994) 101–7.

Beale, G. K. *Union with the Resurrected Christ: Eschatological New Creation and New Testament Biblical Theology.* Grand Rapids: Baker Academic, 2023.

Block, Daniel I. *For the Glory of God: Recovering a Biblical Theology of Worship.* Grand Rapids: Baker Academic, 2014.

Boone, R. Jerome. "Pentecostal Worship and Hermeneutics: Engagement with the Spirit." *Journal of Pentecostal Theology* 26.1 (2017) 110–24.

Bruce, F. F. *Book of Acts.* New International Commentary on the New Testament. Rev. ed. Grand Rapids: Eerdmans, 1988.

Cartledge, Mark. *Charismatic Glossolalia: An Empirical-Theological Study.* New York: Ashgate, 2002.

———. *The Mediation of the Spirit: Interventions in Practical Theology.* Grand Rapids: Eerdmans, 2015.

———. *Testimony in the Spirit: Rescripting Ordinary Pentecostal Theology.* New York: Routledge, 2016.

Carroll, Lewis. *Through the Looking Glass and What Alice Found There.* New York: Penguin Random House, 2010.

Carson, D. A. *Praying with Paul: A Call to Spiritual Reformation.* Grand Rapids: Baker, 2015.

Chan, Simon. *Pentecostal Theology and the Christian Spiritual Tradition.* Eugene, OR: Wipf & Stock, 2000.

———. *Spiritual Theology: A Systematic Study of the Christian Life.* Downers Grove, IL: InterVarsity, 2009.

Coulter, Dale M. "The Whole Gospel for the Whole Person: Ontology, Affectivity, and Sacramentality." *Pneuma* 35.2 (2013) 157–61.

Cox, Harvey. "Jazz and Pentecostalism." *Archives de Sciences Sociales Des Religions* 38.84 (1993) 181–88. http://www.jstor.org/stable/30127247.

Dunning, Benjamin H. *Aliens and Sojourners: Self as Other in Early Christianity.* Philadelphia: University of Pennsylvania Press, 2009.

Faupel, D. William. *The Everlasting Gospel: The Significance of Eschatology in the Development of Pentecostal Thought.* Blandford Forum, UK: Deo, 2019.

Fee, Gordon D. *God's Empowering Presence: The Holy Spirit in the Letters of Paul.* Peabody, MA: Hendrickson, 1995.

———. *Gospel and Spirit: Issues in New Testament Hermeneutics.* Grand Rapids: Baker, 1991.

———. *The First Epistle to the Corinthians.* New International Commentary on the New Testament. Grand Rapids: Eerdmans, 2014.

Fee, Gordon D., and Douglas Stuart. *How to Read the Bible for All Its Worth.* 4th ed. Grand Rapids: Zondervan Academic, 2014.

Félix-Jäger, Steven. *Spirit of the Arts: Towards a Pneumatological Aesthetics of Renewal.* New York: Palgrave Macmillan, 2017.

Harris, Murray J. *Slave of Christ: A New Testament Metaphor for Total Devotion to Christ.* Downers Grove, IL: InterVarsity, 2001.

Hoekema, Anthony A. *The Bible and the Future.* Grand Rapids: Eerdmans, 1994.

Hough, Lula Bell. "Missionary Travels, S. China." *Pentecostal Evangel,* April 21, 1934, pp. 8–9. Courtesy of the Flower Pentecostal Heritage Center.

Hull, Bill. *The Complete Book of Discipleship: On Being and Making Followers of Christ.* Carol Stream, IL: Tyndale, 2014.

Humphrey, Edith M. *Grand Entrance: Worship on Earth as in Heaven.* Grand Rapids: Baker, 2011.

Hunter, Harold D. *Spirit Baptism: A Pentecostal Alternative.* Eugene, OR: Wipf & Stock, 2009.

Kaiser, Walter C., Jr., and Moises Silva. *Introduction to Biblical hermeneutics: The Search for Meaning.* Grand Rapids: Zondervan Academic, 2009.

Kärkkäinen Veli-Matti. *Introduction to Ecclesiology: Ecumenical, Historical, and Global Perspectives,* Downers Grove, IL: IVP Academic, 2002.

———. *Pneumatology: The Holy Spirit in Ecumenical, International, and Contextual Perspective.* Grand Rapids: Baker, 2018.

———. "Mission in Pentecostal Theology." *International Review of Mission* 107.1 (2018) 5–22.

Keener, Craig. *Miracles Today: The Supernatural Work of God in the Modern World.* Grand Rapids: Baker, 2021.

———. *Spirit Hermeneutics: Reading Scripture in Light of Pentecost.* Grand Rapids: Eerdmans, 2016.

Keller, Timothy. *Prayer: Experiencing Awe and Intimacy with God.* London: Penguin, 2016.

Land, Steven Jack. *Pentecostal Spirituality: A Passion for the Kingdom.* Cleveland, TN: CPT, 2010.

Laurito, Timothy. *Speaking in Tongues: A Multidisciplinary Defense.* Eugene, OR: Wipf & Stock, 2021.

Lewis, C. S. *Mere Christianity*. New York: HarperCollins, 2001.

———. *The Silver Chair*. New York: HarperCollins, 2005.

Macchia, Frank D. *Baptized in the Spirit: A Global Pentecostal Theology*. Grand Rapids: Zondervan, 2006.

———. "The Question of Tongues as Initial Evidence: A Review of Initial Evidence, Edited by Gary B. McGee." *Journal of Pentecostal Theology* 1.2. (1993) 117–27.

———. *Tongues of Fire: A Systematic Theology of the Christian Faith*. Eugene, OR: Wipf & Stock, 2023.

Mather, Hannah R. K. *The Interpreting Spirit: Spirit, Scripture, and Interpretation in the Renewal Tradition*. Eugene, OR: Wipf & Stock, 2020.

McClung, Grant. "Truth on Fire: Pentecostals and an Urgent Missiology." 1985. https://digitalshowcase.oru.edu/tren/1123.

McGowan, Andrew B. *Ancient Christian Worship: Early Church Practices in Social, Historical, and Theological Perspective*. Grand Rapids: Baker Academic, 2014.

Menzies, Robert P. *Pentecost: This Is Our Story*. Springfield, MO: Gospel, 2013.

Menzies, William. "The Methodology of Pentecostal Theology: An Essay on Hermeneutics." In *Essays on Apostolic Themes*, edited by Paul Ebert, 1–14. Peabody, MA: Hendrickson, 1985.

Naugle, David K. *Worldview: The History of a Concept*. Grand Rapids: Eerdmans, 2002.

Nel, Marius. "Attempting to Define a Pentecostal Hermeneutics." *Scriptura: Journal for Contextual Hermeneutics in Southern Africa* 114.1 (2015) 1–21.

Oliverio, L. William. *Pentecostal Hermeneutics in the Late Modern World: Essays on the Condition of Our Interpretation*. Eugene, OR: Wipf & Stock, 2022.

Phillips, W. Gary, William E. Brown, and John Stonestreet. *Making Sense of Your World: A Biblical Worldview*. Salem, WI: Sheffield, 2009.

Pinnock, Clark H. "13. The Work of the Spirit in the Interpretation of Holy Scripture from the Perspective of a Charismatic Biblical Theologian." In *Pentecostal Hermeneutics*, edited by Lee Roy Martin, 233–48. Leiden: Brill, 2013.

Polkinghorne, John C. *Science and Providence: God's Interaction with the World*. Ukraine: Templeton, 2011.

Pomerville, Paul A. *The Third Force in Missions: A Pentecostal Contribution to Contemporary Mission Theology*. Peabody, MA: Hendrickson, 2016.

Purdy, Harlyn Graydon. *A Distinct Twenty-First Century Pentecostal Hermeneutic*. Eugene, OR: Wipf & Stock, 2015.

Purtill, Richard. "Defining Miracles." In *In Defense of Miracles a Comprehensive Case for God's Action in History*, edited by R. Douglas Geivett and Gary R. Habermas. Downers Grove, IL: InterVarsity, 2014.

Ramm, Bernard. *The Witness of the Spirit: An Essay on the Contemporary Relevance of the Internal Witness of the Holy Spirit*. Eugene, OR: Wipf & Stock, 2011.

Richie, Tony. *Essentials of Pentecostal Theology: An Eternal and Unchanging Lord Powerfully Present & Active by the Holy Spirit*. Eugene, OR: Wipf & Stock, 2020.

Segler, Franklin M., and Randall Bradley. *Christian Worship: Its Theology and Practice*. Nashville: B&H, 2006.

Smith, C. Fred. *Developing a Biblical Worldview: Seeing things God's way*. Nashville: B&H, 2015.

Smith, James K. A. *Desiring the Kingdom: Worship, Worldview, and Cultural Formation*. Grand Rapids: Baker Academic, 2009.

———. *Thinking in Tongues: Pentecostal Contributions to Christian Philosophy.* Grand Rapids: Eerdmans, 2010.

Stephenson, Christopher A. *Types of Pentecostal Theology: Method, System, Spirit.* New York: Oxford University Press, 2013.

Stephenson, Lisa P. "Pentecostalism and Experience: History, Theology, and Practice." *Journal of Pentecostal Theology* 28.2 (2019) 186–201.

Stronstad, Roger. *The Prophethood of All Believers: A Study in Luke's Charismatic Theology.* Cleveland, TN: CPT, 2010.

Vondey, Wolfgang. *Pentecostal Theology: Living the Full Gospel.* London: Bloomsbury, 2017.

———. "Soteriology at the Altar: Pentecostal Contributions to Salvation as Praxis." *Transformation* 34.3(2017) 223–38.

Warren, E. Janet. "'Spiritual Warfare': A Dead Metaphor?" *Journal of Pentecostal Theology* 21.2 (2012) 278–97.

Warrington, Keith. *Pentecostal Theology: A Theology of Encounter.* New York: T. & T. Clark, 2008.

Wenk, Matthis. "Spiritual Gifts: Manifestation of the Kingdom of God." In *The Routledge Handbook of Pentecostal Theology*, edited by Wolfgang Vondey, 301–10. Abingdon, Oxfordshire: Routledge, 2020.

Willard, Dallas, "Discipleship." In *The Oxford Handbook of Evangelical Theology*, edited by Gerald McDermott, 236–46. Oxford: Oxford University Press, 2010.

———. *The Spirit of the Disciplines: Understanding How God Changes Lives.* San Franscisco: HarperCollins, 1990.

Williams, John Rodman. *Renewal Theology: Systematic Theology from a Charismatic Perspective.* San Franscisco: HarperCollins, 1995.

Yong, Amos. *Discerning the Spirit(s): A Pentecostal-Charismatic Contribution to Christian Theology of Religions.* Eugene, OR: Wipf & Stock, 2019.

———. *Mission after Pentecost: The Witness of the Spirit from Genesis to Revelation.* Grand Rapids: Baker Academic, 2019.

———. *The Missiological Spirit: Christian Mission Theology in the Third Millennium Global Context.* Cambridge, UK: James Clarke, 2014.

———. *Renewing Christian Theology: Systematics for a Global Christianity.* Waco, TX: Baylor University Press, 2014.

———. *The Spirit Poured Out on All Flesh: Pentecostalism and the Possibility of Global Theology.* Grand Rapids: Baker Academic, 2005.